Beyond Engagement

How to Make Your Business an Idea Factory

COREY ROSEN

The National Center for Employee Ownership
Oakland, California

Beyond Engagement

Corey Rosen

Book design by Scott Rodrick

ISBN: 978-1-938220-72-2

The National Center for Employee Ownership
1629 Telegraph Ave., Suite 200
Oakland, CA 94612
Phone: 510-208-1300
Fax: 510-272-9510
Web: www.nceo.org

Contents

Preface

This book draws on 40 years of research, meetings, conversations, conferences, and visits. I have had the privilege of working with hundreds of great ESOP companies. I have been taught, inspired, and moved by the commitment they have made to creating effective high-involvement companies. Many of them have become national models with an impact far beyond their employees and communities.

As a researcher, I am always reminded of Joseph Blasi's wise words. Blasi, a professor at Rutgers, has been a friend and colleague for that same 40 years, and his work has led the field in helping understand what makes employee ownership work. Both of us are committed to serious empirical analysis, but as Joseph put it, analysis of data is ultimately just advanced storytelling.

This book will review the data, but it is mostly storytelling, the stories these companies have written that teach all of us how to make employee ownership work.

The book focuses on finding ways to generate ideas from employees. An appendix has ideas on communicating the ESOP. A much more detailed exploration of that can be found in our ESOP Communications Sourcebook.[1]

I am immensely grateful for all of the generous amounts of time people involved in this book have provided to tell their stories, and hope you are as inspired by them as I am.

---

1. See www.nceo.org/r/sourcebook.

CHAPTER 1

Introduction

Hypertherm is a 100% ESOP-owned, 1,400-employee global company that manufactures plasma cutting tools. It has doubled employment in just the last 10 years. Each year, through its team-based employee involvement system, it generates about 2,000 well-developed ideas, of which about 1,500 are implemented. Imagine if in your company, every year, you got at least one good idea, from every employee, that made your company better. How much stronger would your company be?

Hypertherm and the other companies highlighted in this book understand that the key to successful ownership culture is employee involvement. It's really very simple:

> *The most effective employee ownership companies are the ones that generate and use the most good ideas from the most people about the most different things that can make the company better.*

Research has confirmed this seemingly obvious conclusion. But as obvious as it is, a culture that not only allows and encourages employee idea generation, but bakes that process into its structure of work, is still not the norm in most employee ownership companies and is even less the norm in conventional companies.

A 2017 Gallup poll, for instance, found that only three in 10 employees strongly agree with the statement that their opinions seem to count at work. Gallup calculated that by "moving the ratio to six in 10 employees, organizations could realize a 27% reduction in turnover, a 40% reduction in safety incidents, and a 12% increase in productivity."

As Alan Robinson and Dean Schroeder write in their seminal book *Ideas Are Free,* "Every day, all over the world, millions of working people see problems and opportunities that their managers do not. With little chance to do anything about them, they are forced to watch helplessly as their organizations disappoint and lose customers, and miss opportunity after opportunity that to them are too apparent. The result is performance far lower than it should be and employees who do not respect or trust management and who are not fully engaged in their work."

This book is meant to help your company create and sustain an ownership culture like Hypertherm's. Each chapter discusses general principles, provides working model examples from ESOP companies, and summarizes key takeaways.

Creating ownership cultures is hard work, but it is work that is essential for success.

How Do We Know High-Involvement Culture Drives Employee Ownership Performance?

To get your ESOP to drive performance, the first step is to find ways to make employees care about being owners. So pause a moment and think about what would make that more likely.

Here is what people often tell us:

- Effective communications that explain what a great benefit the ESOP is.
- Showing how what employees do relates to how the company and their stock accounts do.
- Time—you need the ESOP to be around for a while to resonate.
- Demographics—more educated, higher income employees will care more.
- Millennials won't relate well to ESOPs.
- Account values—the higher, the better.

- Size of the annual contribution.
- Industry—ESOPs work best in certain kinds of companies.
- Open-book management.
- How much of the company the ESOP owns.
- Whether employees have voting rights.

But extensive research tells us that these are not the most important factors, and often are not factors at all. Frequent communications, open-book management, and a significant annual contribution matter, but some things that do not matter (once you control for other factors) are industry, demographics (yes, even with millennials), the age of the plan, and whether the plan provides voting rights. What matters the most, both for employee attitudes and the impact of ESOPs on company performance, is the degree to which employees can contribute ideas on a regular basis. In other words, it is the companies that structure ways to generate the most ideas from the most people that really see a difference.

Note that I am not talking about employee engagement, a term much bandied about by management gurus. Sure, you want engaged employees, employees who care about doing their jobs well. But there is a big difference between engagement and involvement. When I watch the Golden State Warriors in a playoff game, I am fully engaged—but not involved. Even if I had some useful idea, no one would listen (nor should they in this case). Engaged employee-owners also are watching the score closely and care a lot about winning, but to create a truly great ownership culture, you need to get them involved in generating ideas and making decisions.

Why is that kind of employee involvement so important to ownership outcomes? Communications around the ESOP and the size of the benefit are both related to the long-term financial benefit of the plan. That is a great and important benefit but (as you no doubt already have discovered) not a day-to-day motivator for most people. By contrast, your role in the company and whether you are really being treated like an owner are day-to-day motivators. Being able to share your ideas, have a meaningful say in how your job is done, and have a direct impact on how well the company—and thus your colleagues—do, are what truly motivate people day to day. Being an ESOP company means I am treated like an owner not just financially but in terms of how my work is done.

These conclusions are not simply based on anecdotes. Back in the 1980s, Katherine Klein (now a professor at Wharton) and I (Corey Rosen) at the NCEO did extensive surveys of employee ownership companies to see what factors were related to how employees viewed their ESOP. Communications and the size of the annual contribution were related to improved attitudes, but the most important factor was how much influence employees had over day-to-day work issues. The results we found were surprising to a lot of people (at the time most people thought communications was what mattered and high-involvement management was not the norm in ESOP companies), but they have been confirmed over and over again in multiple large studies, including a massive study of companies that applied for the Best Places to Work awards from 2005 through 2007. In part because of this work, high-involvement management is much more common in ESOPs today.

You can see how we measured involvement—and get a good visual idea of what an involvement culture does—in the matrix in table 1-1. The shaded area is the sweet spot for employee involvement, where employees have a meaningful say over issues concerning how their jobs are organized and performed. Companies where employees landed often in that sweet spot had the most committed, engaged employees and the lowest turnover.

But does having this level of influence make a difference in how companies perform? Employees might like their work, but does this make the company stronger or weaker, as proponents of more traditional management would have argued years ago?

In 1986, Michael Quarrey and I looked at the performance of a group of employee ownership companies for the five-year period before they set up their ESOP and the five years after. They indexed out market effects by looking at how well employee ownership companies did relative to competitors in the pre- and post-ESOP periods, then subtracted the difference. For example, if a company were growing 3% per year faster than its competitors in the pre-ESOP period, and 5.8% per year faster in

Table 1-1. The employee involvement index

	How much say do employees have over the following issues?				
	No say	Can provide input into work-level decisions	Can make specific recommendations to management directly or through teams	Can make decisions jointly with management	Can make decisions without management approval
Social events					
Working conditions					
Work organization and processes					
Product development					
Strategic policy					
Personnel decisions					

the post-ESOP period, there would be a +2.8 percentage-point difference attributable to the ESOP, other things being equal.

We found that ESOP companies had sales growth rates 3.4% per year higher and employment growth rates 3.8% per year higher in the post-ESOP period than would have been expected based on pre-ESOP performance. But when the companies were divided into three groups based on how participatively managed they were, only the most participative companies showed a gain (these were the companies in the sweet spot of the matrix). These companies grew 8% to 11% per year faster than they would have been expected to grow, while the middle group did about the same, and the bottom group showed a decline in performance. The results were published in the September/October 1987 *Harvard Business Review.*

Subsequent research has confirmed this. The biggest study ever looked at the 780 firms that applied to the "100 Best Companies to Work for in America" competition from 2005 to 2007. All had over 1,000 employees and collectively employed over 6 million people. There were 305,339 employees surveyed. The data included both extensive survey results from 200-300 randomly chosen workers within each company and a workplace culture assessment conducted by the Great Place to Work Institute for 400 of the companies. The researchers also gathered financial performance data on the roughly half of the companies in the group that were publicly traded.

One-sixth of the companies, or about 17%, had an ESOP and 9.1% were majority employee owned. ESOPs had no significant independent effect on return on equity, but the combination of ESOPs with employee involvement was 3.9% greater than for firms without this combination. Involvement alone, however, also had no significant impact. In other words, there is synergy between employee involvement and employee ownership. One without the other is not very effective.

This is a critical point. Some skeptics about employee ownership might argue that all that is needed is for employees to have a "sense of ownership." If a company puts high-involvement practices in place, it doesn't really need to share actual ownership to see results, they argue. I'd like to take these people to lunch—let them pick the spot, soak up the atmosphere, suggest what to eat, and smell the aromas, but not actually get to eat. After all, a sense of lunch should suffice.

Participation without ownership has a similar effect. It can get people interested and engaged for a while, but ultimately employees and managers back off. There are a few reasons for this:

- It becomes difficult to talk about using the numbers to build company value if a large majority of the added value employees create (and often all of it) goes to someone else.
- Managers and supervisors can be protective of what they see as their authority, and worry that these high-involvement practices can diminish it. If employees are owners, however, it is harder not to grant them the right to have some input, and managers and supervisors stand to gain the most from stock value growth.
- Top-level management changes more often lead to changes in culture if companies are not employee owned. Cultural fit is rarely the key factor boards consider in selecting new top leadership in non-ESOP companies, but it is a major factor in ESOP companies.

In the 1990s, we at the NCEO tested this issue by studying the impact of open-book management. We found that companies with both ESOPs and open-book management showed about twice as much incremental growth after adopting open-book management as those that did not share ownership. But what was more telling was that it was very difficult to find companies that started an open-book system that lasted long enough (three years) for the study period to be valid without either dropping it or becoming employee owned.

Today, few people inside or outside the ESOP community would argue that high-involvement management practices are not better than more traditional alternatives. But while people agree with the idea, that often does not translate into structured work practices. This book is intended to help companies find those practices that work for them. (Sadly, few people outside the employee ownership world understand why sharing ownership is a necessary complement to these practices.)

How to Get There

So if you want to build an effective ownership culture company, how do you get there?

Stephen Johnson is an acclaimed thinker about how ideas have changed the world. In his book *Where Good Ideas Come From,* he writes that good ideas take time to incubate. Most good ideas follow the concept of the "adjacent possible." They are the ideas that take you a step or two or three from where you are now, but not so far away that they are hard to implement with the resources you have available. These are not usually eureka moments, but the result of a process. "Good ideas," he says, "come from many small ideas that are given space to interact through systems of human connectedness."

Elixir guitar strings, made by employee-owned W.L. Gore and Associates, is a good example. John Allen, a technical engineer for Gore, tells the story on the Elixir Strings website.

"Gore encourages 'dabble time,'" he says, "where associates take time to think about problem-solving or creating products of value. Some of our engineers were working on push-pull cables for Disney animatronics, using these long cables to animate the movements of the characters. The cables were difficult to handle, so one of the applications/solutions was to make a smoother, lower friction push-pull cable. The engineers were looking at guitar strings as a way to prototype that idea—because they needed something very thin and very strong. Once the strings were integrated into that process, engineering a long-lasting, great-sounding guitar string became a new goal." Guitar strings were a long way from the markets Gore was producing, but a team was formed to investigate whether the idea would work. They enlisted sales, marketing, technical, and engineering people who volunteered to work on the project—and a Gore guitarist. It took three years to figure it out. Few companies would have tolerated that kind of risk-taking. Management was not even involved (at Gore, you don't have to ask, as described in more detail later). The team finally came up with a working product, and Elixir is now a leader in the market—and no wonder, Elixir strings last three times as long as the other leading strings.

But you don't have to be a W.L. Gore, with its thousands of highly educated employees, to be an innovator. The Barclay Water Management Iclor case on the next page explains how it used a high-involvement process to create new product innovations.

Creating the System of Connectedness that Generates Ideas

If Johnson is right, how do you create the system of connectedness in an ESOP company that gets you the kind of idea generation of a Barclay or Hypertherm? We will explore most of the concepts in this chapter and in detail in chapters on each step, but we can outline the general ideas here.

But before doing that, understand that this is hard work most of the time. You will have breakthroughs like Elixir and Iclor, but there will likely be many more missteps. You'll try an approach and find it needs tweaking—or doesn't work at all. You might start an involvement process and find most of the ideas employees generate are about things like more days off or cleaner bathrooms. Mid-level management may be reluctant to move to this new system, and some employees will be skeptical. It will take many months or even longer to get it right, and once you do, people's involvement skills will have advanced and the old processes will need to be replaced.

Similarly, management needs a strong stomach. It takes courage to let people fail, knowing that failing is one of the best ways to learn to do it better next time. It takes courage not to challenge ideas that come to you that you think are probably wrong because you know that if you do that too much, you will stifle any new ideas at all. And it takes courage to know that just because you think you are right does not mean you are.

It is this difficulty that makes genuine high-involvement management still a rarity, but the leaders who take these steps almost never turn back.

Finally, leaders need to understand that high-involvement management does not diminish their authority; it expands it. If you are spending a lot of your time getting involved in the decisions of people at lower

The Adjacent Possible at Barclay

Barclay Water Management is a 100% ESOP-owned company in Waltham, Massachusetts. Barclay's core business is providing chemicals to prevent corrosion in water pipes in buildings. One day, a hospital client asked if Barclay could help them test and treat water for Legionella bacteria. It wasn't a product Barclay had, but the salesperson took the issue back to the lab to see if anything could be done. The lab technicians said they could use existing technologies and chemistry they already had to build a machine to test and treat the water. The product they developed turned out to be much more efficient and provide much better data than what was available. A team of employees developed the next steps and began building and marketing the "Iclor monochloramine solution" to hospitals in the Northeast, and the product quickly became a substantial part of Barclay's business and profits. When Legionnaires' disease hit New York City a couple of years later, Barclay was ready. Its product not only made money, but saved lives.

The Iclor was an adjacent possible that became reality for three reasons:

- Barclay employee-owners were empowered by management to move forward on this on their own initiative.
- The idea built on—but also stepped away from—existing business approaches.
- A team of people from different areas—sales, service, and the lab—worked together to develop the product and its marketing.

Barclay's CEO at the time, Bill Brett, said that in a conventional, top-down company, it is unlikely this would have ever happened. It was a major endeavor initiated from below, not above, and top management probably never would have known about the opportunity because employees wouldn't have told them.

levels of the organization, you are not spending your time focusing on the things that you are best at, the tasks that other people in the organization cannot do as well and, probably, that you most like to do.

Some of the key issues you need to consider in moving from just having an ESOP to having an active system of idea generation follow.

1. Working Harder Is Not Enough

In the early stages of ESOPs, and still for many companies today, there is a base assumption that if you effectively communicate what a good deal the ESOP is, employees will respond with more effort and that will make you more money. While this may be true, it often is true in a relatively inconsequential way.

Let's assume that your communication program succeeds in getting people more motivated. Now let's do the math. We want to figure out:

- What percentage of your employees will work harder? If you are a good company already, probably a lot of your workforce is already working as hard as they can, and some smaller percentage is just incorrigibly not so great.
- How much of your costs are affected by extra effort? Many of your costs—taxes, equipment, leases, marketing, R&D, etc., are not affected by how much harder people work.
- How much harder will those who are susceptible to change work? The structure of your work flow may mean that there are not opportunities to do more, but aside from that, can you expect another 15 minutes a day? Thirty minutes?

Say the answer to 1 is 40% (probably a high estimate, but we'll go with it). The answer to 2 averages about 20% to 35% in most companies. Let's use 30%. Finally, let's be wildly optimistic and say you can get another 60 minutes a day out of those whose behavior might change (12.5% of the day). So:

.4 from harder work
x .3 from costs affected by extra effort
x .125 from an extra 60 minutes a day in work
= 1.5% decrease in costs

A 1.5% decrease in costs is a good thing, and congratulations for getting there. But new ideas can generate much more profitability with the same effort.

2. Great Communications on Their Own Won't Create Great New Ideas

If employees really do understand that their ideas matter, won't they share them if they know how important they are and how much their ESOP account balances depend on them? Or won't they just take the initiative and use the new ideas on their own? Some will, but the research and our experience tell us the very large majority won't.

Employees might know how the ESOP works and how better performance at work will improve the bottom line and stock value. But if an employee has an idea, what does he or she do with it? Can they implement on their own without asking? And if not, who do they ask? Will they just get feedback from an often busy supervisor? Can they discuss it with colleagues? And if they agree, then what? It is all just too ambiguous.

3. Open Doors Are Not Enough

Does your company have an "open-door" policy? Chances are it does. In fact, do you know any companies with official "closed-door" policies? The truth is, almost every company says it has an open-door policy. The problem is that not many people walk through that door. To be sure, some open-door policies are mere rhetoric. Management really doesn't expect employees to stand at their door, wouldn't have the time for them if they did, and wouldn't know exactly what to do with what the employees suggested anyway. But it sounds good. And most companies are sincere. Senior leaders really do expect employees to take advantage of management's genuine interest in employee ideas. Still, very few employees walk through the door.

Why? Well, put yourself in the shoes of an employee. Let's see. Do I leave my machine or my desk to go talk to the boss? Won't that cause a problem? And if I do go, when? How do I know the boss will be there? What if I go and the boss says "We've tried that before"? Or "I'll get back to you"—but never does? Or takes credit for my idea? Or, even worse, makes a big deal about my idea to my colleagues, who now accuse me of apple polishing?

For all these reasons, open-door policies are very rarely enough to create a genuinely participative environment in which employees feel not just that they can share ideas and information, but that it is part of their job to do so. The key is not just to allow employee participation, but to structure it into work routines and expect it as part of everyone's job requirement. Participation is not just a right of ownership; it is a responsibility as well. The articles in this section will talk more about various structures companies have used that have worked.

Open-door policies should not be abandoned, however, even if they are not in themselves enough. When employees do walk through an open door, a few practices can help encourage others to do so. First, if managers are often tied up in meetings or other tasks, make sure there are times when management is specifically available for employees. It's not unlike college professors posting office hours. Second, make sure that any suggestions result either in a detailed explanation of why the idea might not work or, if further consideration is needed, exactly what will happen next and when—and then follow through. Third, it makes sense to try to find something in the idea that is worth pursuing, even if it is just a piece of the proposal. Finally, don't assume that management always knows best. It's worth taking a risk on some ideas management does not agree with, even just to show that employee ideas are taken seriously.

Some sobering data: in our ownership culture survey, we consistently find that managers believe employees can share their ideas and get them acted on much more than employees think they can. So don't confuse what you want to happen with what is happening.

4. Good Ideas Require Good Information

Employee ideas are great, but they shouldn't be formed in an information vacuum. Employees need to evaluate how their new ideas will affect the critical measurements of performance the ideas are meant to improve. They also need the broader context of how these numbers affect the overall bottom line.

Companies that follow these practices create metrics for all employee teams. These will vary widely. They may be measures of quality control, customer satisfaction, margin improvement, sales increases, overhead absorption, cost savings, improved productivity, new product development, etc. In most cases, several numbers will be tracked, posted, and discussed on a regular basis. Sharing numbers in this way not only improves ideas, but gives people a greater sense of ownership. And the numbers create a game atmosphere in the company that can be motivating in its own right.

5. Move from Permission to Structure

The next step is to move from permitting ideas to structuring a process to develop them. Generating ideas should be seen as a core responsibility of all employees, and creating workable structures a core responsibility of leadership.

This will take many forms, as explored in chapter 5, "Work-Level Teams." Structures involve ways for employees to talk to one another to identify and solve problems, and often to implement solutions. These can include functional teams, ad hoc committees, cross-functional teams, self-managing teams, idea systems processes for sharing ideas remotely, and other approaches.

To make a structured process work, you need to focus on several key principles:

- Identifying problems is more important than identifying solutions.
- Identifying and implementing good solutions depends on using the right metrics.

- Responsibility should be clear. Employees should not face ambiguity about what they are allowed to discuss, resolve, and implement.
- Get the right people on the right teams.
- Create psychological safety.
- Make sure there is time to do this. "Lean" can be great, but if people feel too stressed by other obligations, they won't take these processes seriously.

We will discuss the specifics of making teams work in chapter 5, mentioned above.

6. Get Management Buy-In

None of this will work unless top management is committed to it and shows it in very specific ways. This can include just talking about its importance, but far better is showing it through celebrating new ideas in a newsletter and meetings, evaluating leaders at all levels on how well they support ideas systems, and providing clear and permissive guidance on how much the committees and teams can do on their own without management approval. Don Carney, the CEO at Barclay, told employees to act on any ideas costing less than $5,000; if it is more, employees ask, but they understand that answers will almost certainly be yes even if Carney is skeptical. Carney's view is that employees will learn from their mistakes and that, in any event, their judgment may be better than his anyway because they are closer to the issues. Nothing will kill employee idea generation faster than a management that says it wants ideas but then acts slowly or negatively on them.

How to Create Your Ideas Structure

Finally, how do you get this all going? Our recommendation is to form an ideas team. Ideally, the team is made up of people who are not part of senior management. They may be elected by their peers or appointed by management, but most often the team will be created through a process of some people volunteering and some people being asked by management to serve. Teams can vary in size from two to three people to several. In multidivisional companies, there may be teams at each division level and an overall steering committee.

The charge of the team is to create and operate an ideas process. These can take many forms, as examples in subsequent chapters will show. The team should start by getting ideas on how to get ideas. A good place to start is by reading *Ideas Are Free* by Dean Schroeder and Alan Robinson and *The Great Game of Business* by Jack Stack and Bo Burlingham. *Ideas Are Free* is a groundbreaking book showing the power of small ideas, with dozens of examples of how companies do it. *The Great Game of Business* describes the processes for idea generation at SRC Holdings, a 100% ESOP company that many believe has the best developed, most effective system for employee involvement in the ESOP world (or perhaps any world). We will be revisiting SRC often in these pages. The team can also attend ESOP conferences to listen to how companies have created their own ideas processes and can visit nearby ESOP companies.

It is essential that ideas not just be solutions to problems. In fact, it is arguably much more important to be able to identify problems. Knowing the right problems makes finding the right solutions a lot easier. Employees need to know that a great idea can just be to identify an issue they do not know how to solve—but someone else may. Saying "if you don't have a solution to the problem don't bother me" is like saying if you smell a gas leak, don't tell anyone unless you know how to turn it off.

A good second step is to survey employees or do focus group meetings to get employee ideas on how they can play a more effective role. Find out what their roadblocks are when they have good ideas and how they think they might be resolved.

Another way to do this is with an exercise we have often used in presentations. Its steps are below:

The Involvement Exercise

1. Gather employees into a large room set with tables for 6-10 people.
2. Ask the group to designate a reporter.

3. Ask everyone at each table to think (but not say) what would happen if they had an idea. Who would they go to? What is the likely outcome? What prevents them or their colleagues from sharing ideas?
4. Now ask people to take five minutes for each person to briefly report what they came up with.
5. When this is finished, ask the group to discuss which two of the issues are the most important.
6. Repeat steps 2-6, but this time focus on what can be done to make it easier to share ideas and make them happen.
7. Go around the room and have each group report its problems, then go around again and have each group report solutions.

It is important in this process to make sure people are focusing on structural issues, not just "we need to listen better." Structural issues are things like not having time to do it, not having an opportunity to meet as a group to talk about ideas, not having a process where managers have to respond to ideas, etc.

With the research done, the ideas team can now start to experiment with solutions. Some common approaches (to be discussed more later) include:

- Have an ideas forum on the website where people can post ideas or problems, get feedback, and post results. The ideas team needs to then establish a process for how these ideas will be reviewed and how actions will be taken on them.
- Create a specific form (on paper or online) that employees can use to identify a problem. The form can ask employees to describe the issue, identify why it matters, and, if they have a potential solution, suggest it. Again, the ideas team uses the form to decide on the next steps.
- Create a series of ad hoc committees to address issues as they arise, often from one of the first two steps, but also from informal conversations, surveys, and issues raised at staff meetings. Com-

mittees should have people with the relevant knowledge and skills appointed to them but also allow for volunteers.

- Create functional teams based on common tasks that meet on a regular schedule to discuss issues, generate ideas, and make recommendations or take actions.
- Create self-managing teams in key cross-functional areas such as marketing, product development, quality, staff policies, and customer relations.

Teams need to understand that the first initiatives may not work or work as well as hoped. The team needs to reevaluate and make changes as needed. Even successful first steps need revisiting periodically because as people get better at the process, what worked before may need to be changed.

Schroeder and Robinson in *Ideas Are Free* list eight key characteristics of effective ideas processes that can guide the team's approach:

1. Ideas are encouraged and welcomed.
2. Submitting ideas is simple.
3. Evaluation of ideas is quick and effective.
4. Feedback is timely, constructive, and informative.
5. Implementation is rapid and smooth.
6. Ideas are reviewed for additional potential.
7. People are recognized, and success is celebrated.
8. Idea system performance is measured, reviewed, and improved.

Don't Be Intimidated by the Superstars

At our conference in Atlanta in 2017, as we often do, we highlighted great ESOP companies, the kinds of companies you will read about in this book. The idea was, and is, to inspire people to create their own great cultures and to learn strategies from these experienced pros. But some companies, especially those with newer ESOPs and those that had not done much yet with their cultures (but wanted to give it a try) told us they were a bit intimidated. How could they ever get from where they were to where these companies are? It's an understandable concern. These companies are exceptional and hopefully inspirational, but they are the Mount Everest climbers of ESOPs. Maybe you'll just get up the nearest rolling hill for now, but even that journey is likely to make you a much better company than your peers. Any level of higher involvement you can achieve is a win. None of these companies had great ownership cultures when their ESOPs were new. In fact, a common theme was that they struggled for years to really get their cultures off the ground.

The most important thing the team can do is start somewhere. Pick an idea or two and try that. It should be a real change from what you do now, but not so far off as to be too difficult. After all, people don't become marathoners by starting off with a 20-mile weekend jaunt. You might be really lucky and nail the right idea or ideas from day one, but it certainly isn't likely. Most new ideas have mixed success. Evaluate what went right and wrong and tweak the system.

Once you have a system, measure. Find ways to determine if the process is working. That can be better scores on an engagement survey, better quality, higher profits, new customers, and many other outcomes. Measurements should be shared on a regular basis with everyone. Keeping score is itself a motivator for people. We wouldn't be very motivated to play a basketball game if only the coach knew the score. One useful approach is to figure out your critical numbers for each operation.

Finally, make this a management priority, not a sideshow. The great companies say it is their business model. That means that top management needs to show that it puts a high priority on this. Setting up an ESOP is complicated, but not that hard with the right advice. Setting up an ownership culture is conceptually simple—find structured ways for employees to be able to share and implement more ideas—but practically very difficult. It will take time—years, in most cases. It will seem like you are never going to get there. But every year or so when you are thinking about how to take the next steps, look back to see what ground you have covered. Chances are, you will have made some progress. If the process has just generated a few new good ideas, it will be worthwhile. Stay with it, and most companies find that they can become stars too.

KEY TAKEAWAYS

- Communications matter, but what really creates singular performance in employee ownership companies is the generation of more ideas from more people.
- Identifying problems is at least as important as identifying solutions.
- Idea generations rarely comes through an open door. Idea generation happens because you structure it, not because you permit and even encourage it.
- Good ideas require good information. Teach and share overall financials but also work-level key metrics.
- Create an ideas generation process by starting with an ideas team.
- Identify the barriers to idea generation; identify solutions from employee feedback and what you can learn from leading employee ownership companies.
- Make sure management buys in and shows it in concrete ways.

CHAPTER 2

What It Means to Be a Leader in an Ownership Culture Company

To be a leader, you must first be a servant and serve those people who permit you the opportunity to lead.

—Andre Carrier, COO, Eureka Casinos

Being a leader in an ESOP company requires a bit of a missionary streak. While the benefits of being employee owned are significant, it also requires a level of commitment that does not exist in non-ESOP companies. As a result, you really have to believe in the path you are taking, always be ready to discuss your collective "why," and preach that message to stakeholders on regular basis.

—Dan Kenary, CEO, Harpoon Brewery

Being the leader of an ESOP company is completely different than what I expected. Most leaders treat their employees like they are disposable because they are focused on the financial results from the last 90 days and the next 90 days. At Polyguard we are able to look past instant gratification and focus on the best long-term plans for the company and our employee-owners. We treat our employees like owners and they in turn treat the business, our customers, and each other like owners. The level of communication, camaraderie, and teamwork at Polyguard is unlike anything else I have ever experienced. We have had 26 consecutive years of sales growth at Polyguard. That doesn't happen by accident.

—Shawn Eastham, president, Polyguard Products

Ask just about any leader of a successful ESOP company for a quote about what it means to be a leader in an ESOP company, and you will hear common themes. Leading an ESOP company is a lot different than leading a conventional firm. Great employee ownership leaders value their culture first, find ways for employee-owners to have meaningful input into decisions affecting their work and the company, help create and sustain a system of values-based management, focus on the long term, and, above all, are humble enough to know their ideas are not always the best ones. But it is not all just about rights and participation; employee ownership company leaders also demand responsibility from their fellow employee-owners.

Perhaps the ultimate expression of ownership culture leadership can be found at employee- and family-owned W.L. Gore and Associates. The 9,500-employee multinational company is most famous for Gore-Tex©, but it serves very diverse markets by using a special polymer it pioneered to laminate clothing, create medical devices, and produce a variety of industrial devices. It even makes guitar strings, a story we explored earlier. They have been issued more than 2,000 patents, and their products are in more than 40 million medical implant devices. Gore consistently is named one of the best and most innovative places to work in the country.

Gore was created in 1958 by Bill and Vieve Gore. Bill had been an engineer at DuPont and was frustrated by the hierarchy and bureaucracy. His company would be different. There would be no hierarchy, no proliferation of titles, and nothing like traditional management. Employees would be called and considered associates, and rewarded as owners.

The core concept in Gore's innovative process is that it does not define leadership in terms of a spot on the hierarchy—indeed, Gore insists its organization chart has no hierarchy at all, but is a lattice. There is no fixed or assigned authority. There are no bosses—just mentors and sponsors. Natural leadership emerges project by project based on who chooses to follow someone. Tasks and functions are organized through commitments, not someone telling people what to do. In a lattice, each person interacts directly with every other person in the lattice, not through a mediated process of hierarchy.

Mary Tilley, enterprise business transformation leader at Gore, summarized Gore's leadership model this way at the NCEO's annual conference in 2015:

1. You aren't a leader unless you have followers.
2. You don't lead through command and control but through influence.
3. You're measured on both what you deliver and how you deliver it.
4. Decisions are driven through the most knowledgeable associates. This means, among other things, that leadership can shift by project.

Tilley said four key values drive Gore's culture:

1. Belief in the individual: We believe associates are capable and will do what's best for the enterprise.
2. Power of small teams: We believe small teams leverage trust and complementary skills to create great results.
3. Long-term view: We want to be here for a long time and invest for long-term results and not short-term conditions.
4. All in the same boat: We believe what we do individually affects the whole enterprise.

In practice, this means that projects get created at Gore when an associate has an idea and can enlist enough other associates to form a team. The team can then draw down a budget to work on the idea. Only projects that are large and risky enough to endanger the whole company need further approval. Teams select their own leaders, which is why Tilley says leadership shifts by issue. The Gores' most fervently held principle was that leadership should be a function of expertise issue by issue, not job title. That means, Tilley said, that about half of Gore's associates are or will be leaders at some time. Tilley's unusual title reflects this. She is a leader on an issue—working with others, finding ways to continually transform the organization—not someone occupying a fixed hierarchical position.

The Gores never believed that their model would work for every company—leaders have to be willing to make an enormous leap to do this. While many employee ownership companies emulate some aspects of Gore, none goes as far in reconceptualizing leadership so thoroughly. But the core concept of Gore—base leadership on expertise not position and be willing to shift authority by issue, not title—is an aspiration we think all ESOP company leaders should have.

Valuing Culture First

Great employee ownership companies are defined by great cultures. Leaders in great employee ownership companies put culture first and make sure everyone knows it.

Peter Drucker, the legendary management guru, is famous for reputedly having said that "culture eats strategy for breakfast" (although some say he said lunch and the quote never appears in anything he wrote). There are many interpretations of what this means. A poor culture can certainly eat up a good strategy if disengaged employees do little to implement it, or even undermine it. But a great culture might make a so-so strategy work anyway if employees are constantly looking for ways to make it work and improve it. But if your business strategy is to continue to focus on products for a shrinking market, no culture is good enough.

In most discussions of great cultures, the authors talk about how engaged employees eagerly and effectively implement strategies and plans from insightful management. In that most annoying phrase to advocates of actual employee ownership, they urge companies to give employees "a sense of ownership." They don't usually talk much about employees being able to do more than have input into how some work-level decisions are implemented.

But great employee ownership cultures are about a lot more than more engaged compliance and occasional input. They are about creating systems and structures where people don't just feel like owners, but actually take ownership. They understand what is at stake as an owner for themselves and their colleagues. They know the metrics well enough to gauge how what they and their colleagues do affects the bottom line and stock price. They feel a sense of mutual obligation to one another. And, most important, they are empowered to generate and implement new ideas.

Great ownership culture leaders make it a priority to create and sustain these high-involvement cultures. They do that in a number of key ways:

- They make communicating about how the ESOP works an ongoing, employee driven, significant part of work every day.
- They regularly discuss how the company is doing, including challenges and opportunities. Their reports to employees might resemble a summary report to the board.
- They create systems to share financial information at the corporate and work level and provide the time and resources to train people how to understand and use the numbers.
- They create, or, better, let employees create, a system of employee involvement and make that part of work. Managers are partly evaluated on how well they make that happen.
- They create systems for leadership development to ensure that upcoming leaders buy into and practice the same values.

The chapters that follow discuss all of these issues in more depth.

Insisting on Shared Responsibility

In most companies, the employment deal is simple. The manager tells you what to do and you do it. If you do it well, you get to stay and maybe even get a raise or a promotion. "Going the extra mile" is appreciated, at least by your bosses, but maybe not your colleagues, who may see you as raising the bar for them. You are not normally expected to contribute new ideas, much less take the initiative to carry them out. You aren't privy to much information about the company, much less be expected to understand how the metrics affect your job and the company's performance.

It is very different in a great ownership culture company. Now your boss, and often even more your colleagues, expect you to think and act like an owner, to contribute ideas, take responsibility, understand how the company works and makes money, know how your part of the company contributes to that, and work to help your colleagues succeed. Leaders who allow anything other than this in employees lose credibility with employee-owners. As Bill Pickens, former CEO of ESOP-owned Pool Covers used to say, "At Pool Covers, it's be great or be gone."

Amanda DeVito is the vice president of engagement at ESOP-owned Butler/Till, a media and communications agency in Rochester, New York. She has explained this as well as anyone we have heard. She starts by explaining how Butler/Till runs its high-involvement culture. Leaders in an ownership culture company, she says, need to help employees "think through the lens of ownership when they come up with an idea, and come back and tell me how it is fleshed out. The biggest thing about ownership is reminding people of their fiscal responsibility to each other. If they come up with an idea, they need to challenge it to see if it really is in line with the Butler/Till strategy. When they think through the numbers, most times they come back and say it doesn't make sense."

To help them do that, Butler/Till provides employees with all kinds of financial metrics, including internal training programs on using financials. Still, she says, "sometimes you have to let people take risks even if you think it may fail because it is a way to learn. They'll never forget what they learned." That leap of faith can't be taken for projects that have a major cost, but taking these risks is an effective way to teach business lessons and convey to employees that they really are owners.

DeVito says that mid-level leaders need to model ownership behavior by putting together particular goals that align with the vision, then encourage the people they work with to come up with their own ideas. Encouraging employee ideas is essential and is part of performance reviews.

But what if it doesn't work for every employee? Like all leaders, DeVito has to face the challenge of employees who are great at their jobs, but not very good at culture. DeVito sees the issue as a grid:

Job competence	Cultural competence
High	High
High	Low
Low	High
Low	Low

DeVito says the bottom quadrant people need to be compassionately moved out. The people who are high on jobs skills but low on cultural skills need coaching—or maybe a job change or even also to be compassionately moved out if they cannot learn the culture skills. The people with low job skills and good culture skills need training and development. But DeVito says that keeping even very high performing employees who create cultural issues is not worth it—they can be so demoralizing that good people leave.

DeVito is a big fan of the book *The Leadership Challenge* by James Kouzes and Barry Posner. The book lays out five principles of leadership: modeling the way, inspiring a shared vision, challenging the process, enabling others to act, encouraging the heart.

Leaders need to model the behaviors they want others to emulate and set a vision they can follow, she says. They break down goals into smaller interim objectives that can yield regular wins. They are always willing to challenge the process to improve the organization and are willing to take risks to do it. Critically for an ESOP, they enable others to act, eliminating bureaucratic obstacles and hierarchical boundaries that aren't productive. Finally, they "encourage the heart" by recognizing people for what they accomplish—they "make people heroes."

Finding Ways to Make Vision, Mission, and Values Lived Parts of the Company

Look at any company's website and you will see statements of vision, values, and/or mission. Most are pretty anodyne—they want to be the premier provider of high-quality paraphernalia and they seek to value employees and community. Lots of CEOs also insist they "put people first." The statements get put on plaques, websites, and maybe business cards—and then business proceeds as usual. You can even go the web and find a mission generator app.

There are some mission statements at companies that stand out, however, including employee ownership companies. The mission of Southwest Airlines (which is partly owned by a profit-sharing plan invested in company stock) says, "The mission of Southwest Airlines is dedication to the highest quality of Customer Service delivered with a sense of warmth, friendliness, individual pride, and Company Spirit. We are committed to provide our employees a stable work environment with equal opportunity for learning and personal growth. Creativity and innovation are encouraged for improving the effectiveness of Southwest Airlines. Above all, employees will be provided the same concern, respect, and caring attitude within the organization that they are expected to share externally with every Southwest Customer." If you fly Southwest, you probably see this mission actually being lived.

It's a great mission statement because it emphasizes what makes Southwest different from other airlines. Compare it to the generic-sounding mission of American Airlines: "AMR Corporation is committed to providing every citizen of the world with the highest quality air travel to the widest selection of destination possible." If you were an employee, which mission would engage you more?

But crafting a meaningful, well-stated mission is less important than how it is developed and lived. Some ESOP companies take on the first challenge by enlisting employees in the process of developing new statements or rethinking old ones.

Once the mission is in place, making sure it is lived requires feedback. Surveys are one way to see if employees believe the company walks the talk; focus groups are another. Both ways do two things: they help find where you are falling down (if you are) and they give employee-owners the sense that leaders care about whether the mission is more than uplifting verbiage.

A Humble Mindset

One of the things that most immediately strikes people who meet leaders from great ESOP companies is how often they are truly humble. They do not assume that just because they are in a position of authority that what they think is automatically better than what other employee owner thinks. Amy Edmondson, a professor of leadership at Harvard Business School, describes why this matters so much:

> The bottom line is that no one wants to take the interpersonal risk of proposing ideas when the boss appears to think he or she knows everything. A learning mindset, which blends humility and curiosity, mitigates this risk. A learning mindset recognizes that there is always more to learn. Frankly, adopting a humble mindset when faced with the complex, dynamic, uncertain world in which we all work today is simply realism.
>
> The term *situational humility* captures this concept well (the need for humility lies in the situation) and may make it easier for leaders, especially those with abundant self-confidence, to recognize the validity, and the power, of a humble mindset. Keep in mind that confidence and humility are not opposites. Confidence in one's abilities and knowledge, when warranted, is far preferable to false modesty. But humility is not modesty, false or otherwise. Humility is the simple recognition that you don't have all the answers, and you certainly don't have a crystal ball. Research shows that when leaders express humility, teams engage in more learning behavior.[1]

Humble leadership is also the key to creating the sense of psychological safety that enables employee engagement in generating and implementing ideas. Julia Rozovsky is the analyst who headed Google's massive analysis of why its teams worked—or didn't. The results got national attention, perhaps because they did not find that such things as expertise or team composition were the most important elements. Instead, she wrote that

> psychological safety was far and away the most important of the five dynamics we found—it's the underpinning of the other four [dependability, structure, meaning, and impact]. How could that be? Taking a

1. Amy Edmondson, *The Fearless Organization* (Hoboken, NJ: Wiley, 2019).

> risk around your team members seems simple. But remember the last time you were working on a project...Turns out, we're all reluctant to engage in behaviors that could negatively influence how others perceive our competence, awareness, and positivity. Although this kind of self-protection is a natural strategy in the workplace, it is detrimental to effective teamwork.
>
> On the flip side, the safer team members feel with one another, the more likely they are to admit mistakes, to partner, and to take on new roles. And it affects pretty much every important dimension we look at for employees. Individuals on teams with higher psychological safety are less likely to leave Google, they're more likely to harness the power of diverse ideas from their teammates, they bring in more revenue, and they're rated as effective twice as often by executives.[2]

Humble leaders create psychological safety because they are approachable and sincerely believe that everyone can contribute not just their efforts but their ideas—ideas that often are better than theirs.

Amy Edmondson provides a useful framework for building this sense of psychological safety through situational humility (table 2-1).

While it may be easy to describe the mindset that works best, the truth is that most people who rise to managerial levels are good at what they do and are habituated to telling people what to do. To shift to asking people what to do, to be genuinely open to new ideas, and to be willing to take risks on ideas you don't think will work but other people do is not an easy thing to do. This mindset is often easier for top leaders, especially the CEO, than mid-level managers. It is important, therefore, to try to hire new people at this level who have shown these traits in prior employment, while internally promoting people based in significant part on how well they do in encouraging and enabling those they work with to come up with and implement ideas. Top leaders can get started by making a commitment, asking other leaders to do the same, and to try agreeing to ideas that employee teams want to pursue but leaders do not think will be useful. Start with low-risk ideas. If these

2. Julia Rozofsky, "The five keys to a successful Google team," November 17, 2015, https://rework.withgoogle.com/blog/five-keys-to-a-successful-google-team.

end up working, leaders might start to learn that these are risks worth taking and that their ideas may not always be the best ones.

Table 2-1. The leader's toolkit for psychological safety

	Setting the stage	Inviting participation	Responding productively
Leadership tasks	**Frame the work** • Set expectations about failure, uncertainty, and interdependence to clarify the need for voice **Emphasize purpose** • Identify what's at stake, why it matters, and for whom it matters	**Demonstrate situational humility** • Acknowledge gaps **Practice inquiry** • Ask good questions • Model intense listening **Set up structures and processes** • Create forums for input • Provide guidelines for discussion	**Express appreciation** • Listen • Acknowledge and thank **Destigmatize failure** • Look forward • Offer help • Discuss, consider, and brainstorm next steps **Sanction clear violations**
Accomplishes	Shared expectations and meaning	Confidence that voice is welcome	Orientation toward continuous learning

Leadership Succession That Sustains Your Culture

Robert Beyster is one of the most important figures in the history of employee ownership. In 1969, he started Science Applications International Corporation (SAIC) which, by the early 2000s, grew to over 40,000 employees. From the outset, Beyster shared ownership broadly with employees in a variety of ways—stock purchase plans, stock options, and, after ESOPs were created in 1974, an ESOP. SAIC thrived, with steady stock price growth based on a high-involvement, risk-taking, entrepreneurial culture. Beyster was so committed to the idea of employee ownership that he started and substantially funded a foundation to promote it (now part of the Rady School of Business at UC-San Diego).

Beyster eventually brought on an impressive board of directors with top-level financial, defense, and science expertise. While they all paid lip service to the idea of employee ownership and the SAIC culture, it was not where their hearts were. In 2003, he retired and a new CEO was brought in, one who also said he too was committed to the Beyster way of doing business. Sadly, that was not the case. The board and the new CEO decided they should take the company public. The pressures of the day-to-day expectations of the marketplace quickly led to dramatic changes. Employee ownership was deemphasized; traditional management approaches emphasized. In the second edition of his book, *The SAIC Solution: How We Built an $8 Billion Employee-Owned Technology Company,* Beyster says he did not pay adequate attention to the composition of the board or the incoming leadership:

"By the late 90s, I knew that I had a succession issue. The challenge was twofold. On one hand, I knew that maintaining the company's strong leadership and keeping our unique employee culture in place was absolutely critical to SAIC's ongoing and future success. However, it was difficult for me to find the right successor and to wind down my own position of leadership with the company I had founded and poured so much of my working life into . . . . I didn't commit myself to making succession happen, so it didn't happen in a way that would preserve our unique culture."

Given how critical the right kind of leadership is, succession is a make or break issue for companies. So how do you get it right?

In the NCEO issue brief *Leadership Development and Succession* (see www.nceo.org/r/leadership), Amy Lyman, a cofounder of the Great Place to Work Institute (the organization that identifies the Best Companies to Work For in the U.S. and around the world), provided an insightful overview of what needs to be done:

> "The three key activities that founders/leaders need to engage in to support the smooth implementation of leadership development and succession plans promote cultural congruity between current and future leaders. A fourth key activity—structured succession-specific activities—keeps things moving forward yet varies significantly depending on the type of organization, its history, and its resources.

The three founder/current leader activities that support effective leadership development and succession practices include:

- *Defining the organization's culture:* Leaders need to create a clearly articulated statement, inclusive of values and practices, that honestly reflects what they know to be true (for themselves) about how and why the company operates the way it does. This statement needs to be concise and focused, identifying the link between the values in practice and the purpose of the organization.
- *Initiating straightforward conversations:* New leaders need practical guidance in their first three to six months as they get their feet on the ground. This is true for all new leaders, yet especially necessary for leaders who have come from outside the company. Conveying clear practical expectations for strategic and cultural accomplishments during the first six months provides a path for pursuing and evaluating success. What will be asked of a new leader in terms of his or her contributions, for both specific work tasks and responsibility for the culture?
- *Being personally responsible:* Current leaders need to take seriously their responsibility to train, teach, coach, and support new leaders and those in the pipeline. The best role models for behaviors you will see in future leaders are the leaders currently in place. Absent a wholesale shift in a leadership group, the current team will have significant influence over how new members of the group perform.

The fourth activity that is essential to successful leadership succession and development is:

- *Building a recruitment and training platform:* Building a recruitment, selection, and onboarding process with your company's culture in mind will provide the system and structure for all of this to happen. Customizing off-the-shelf approaches also works, yet customizing is essential as your organization's unique culture needs to permeate the entire leadership succession process. New leaders need a clear line of sight between who they are, their specific work roles, why they in particular have been brought in to their new positions, and how they are expected to contribute to and support the culture for the long-term success of the organization.

Many people believe that leadership succession activities should begin with the fourth activity—just get right in to building a recruitment and hiring process that will bring in the best people in the industry. Yet without the work involved in the first three activities, efforts to recruit and hire people to support sustainable growth and profitability in your organization will be mildly successful at best, and in many cases an outright disaster. The likelihood of success increases with the quality and clarity of culture-specific guidance that is provided."

We can look at these principles in action at both the CEO level and for multiple levels below for that.

Succession Below the CEO

First, recognize that succession is not just about the CEO. Every critical position needs a succession plan. Some of the best ESOP companies develop formal plans to do this. Each critical person is asked to identify one or more possible successors and work with them to develop a plan on how they might move into that position should they desire to do that. Conversely, every employee is given the opportunity to plot a career path, with a mentor at the company helping them to identify the skills they need to acquire to get to where they want to go. This may be upward, but it could also be horizontally to a different job. Each year, the mentor (who often is their supervisor) works with them to assess progress. This process not only identifies future leaders, but reinforces the idea of employee ownership—that in this company, employees really can own their future.

For any position that involves managing teams or individuals, a key part of the program is to identify ownership culture skills. Key attributes include:

- Does the individual show openness to new ideas from other people?
- How does the individual encourage other people to share ideas?

- Does the individual treat people fairly?
- Do peers regard the individual as a leader?
- Has the individual shown a focus on improving team performance?
- Does the individual have strong communications skills?

This is all easier when the individual has had some elements of a leadership role. But what if they haven't? In *Leadership Development and Succession* (cited above), Ted Freeman of Praxis suggests looking at how the individual has responded to situations with steep learning curves. Have they waited for issues to come to them, worked through them themselves, or (ideally) sought out involvement from others? If they participate in teams, do others perceive them as a natural leader?

It also helps to provide training in ownership culture leadership. This can include sending people to conferences to listen to stories from other great ESOP companies or Great Game of Business companies developing an internal training program (perhaps with assistance from a consultant specializing in ownership culture), or reading one of the many good books on this topic, particularly the ones we mentioned earlier. You can also develop a leaders discussion group to have regular meetings to share insights and stories.

The most advanced form of this is to develop a formal training program, such as the one at BL Companies, a 100% ESOP. BL provides integrated architecture, engineering, environmental, and land surveying services to public and private clients in the Northeast and Mid-Atlantic states. As Freeman recounted, when BL Company's CEO retired in 2006, there was no formal succession plan in place for the CEO or other leaders. Leaders were well trained in architecture and engineering, but not in the soft skills needed in an ownership culture. Silos separated departments, and leaders had difficulty communicating across them. At a strategic planning meeting, the leaders decided they need to develop a training program that could help identify and train future leaders to fit into an ownership culture.

First, they developed a competency model outlining eight core competencies: accountability, teamwork, developing others, relationship building, client focus, communication, strategic thinking, and leading and managing change, each defined by a series of behaviors. When hiring people, skills in terms of relationship building, listening, and communicating were added to the normal issues evaluated. These were also added to annual reviews. BL developed a two-day learning program to help current and potential leaders develop the kinds of skills that could make them effective in empowering colleagues to share ideas and information. Ultimately, over 50 people participated. Freeman writes that "After going through a learning session, each participant was assigned to a cohort group, which was led by a pair of senior leaders in the company. In monthly cohort group meetings, participants discussed their progress on their action plans; read and discussed books and articles on leadership, management, and organizational behavior; and engaged in in-depth conversations about each of the leadership competencies and how they were (or could be) implemented at the company."

Recology is a 100% employee-owned integrated resource recovery and recycling company. It provides collection, hauling, processing, composting, consulting, and disposal services to homes and businesses in the Western United States. The over 3,000-employee company has multiple locations on the West Coast and has the highest landfill diversion rate in the country through an aggressive program of composting and recycling. It has developed its own thorough succession planning process for multiple levels of the company, the Recology Academy Foundations Program. The program involves 12 to 16 people at a time and targets both those in leadership and those who show promise as potential future leaders. There are nine monthly one-day sessions. There are opportunities to learn more about the company, do community service, discuss leadership skills, independent projects students take on to improve the high-involvement process at Recology, shadowing leaders, and other learning opportunities. There is a more immersive program for those who are likely to become senior leaders. Topics covered include advanced communication skills, developing others, team dynamics, organizational culture, ways to promote employee participation, strategic thinking and planning, and other key skills. Recology's formal succession plans cover over 50 positions in the company.

Some companies, such as SRC Holdings, take these programs even further and develop them for every employee. Employees in any critical position are required to have a succession plan, and all other employees have a career plan. Leaders work with all those who report to them to review their plan each year and provide feedback on what skills they need to develop to move up or into a different job. This company-wide approach creates a compelling sense of agency and ownership for anyone willing to take on the challenge.

CEO Succession

Ownership cultures are almost invariably driven in large part by the CEO. The CEO can set the tone and expectations for a genuinely high-involvement culture, or undermine it by just paying lip service to the idea. So how do you identify people to replace the CEO who will be great ownership culture promoters?

Ideally, succession will come from within. Hiring outside CEOs is sometimes necessary, but risky, as the Beyster experience shows. People smart enough to be considered for a CEO position are also probably smart enough to figure out how they need to answer interview questions about their approach to ownership culture. A board may think it has just the right person only to be disappointed later.

There are steps that can help. First, make sure there are conversations with other people in the firm the candidates would be leaving that focus on how the individual related to other employees. Were they genuinely open to ideas that were not their own? Did they invite new ideas from people at all levels, and, if so, how specifically did they do that? Were they willing to go with an idea not their own even if they were in a position to do so, and did they share metrics with other employees? Ask the candidates themselves to relate several specific stories about how they set up systems to generate ideas from other people and what they did with them. If possible, hire a potential new CEO to work in the company for one or more years to learn more about how the person might work out.

While the board and the top leadership should interview finalists, also consider having nonmanagement employees, such as members of the ESOP committee or the ideas team, do their own interviews. Not only can this give you a sense of how the candidate relates to people at this level, but it is another confirmation of your own ownership culture.

If you can promote from within, however, this is far better. The potential candidates have track records on how they act within an ownership culture. One approach to selecting a candidate I have used successfully as an ESOP company board member is to have outside board members set up a series of interviews, typically with about 10-15 people one-on-one for about 10 minutes each, asking who they see as potential CEOs and why. The employees should know this is only advisory; the board ultimately will make its own decision. But in each of three cases, the process narrowed down the field to one or two people, and those new leaders turned out to be great fits for the culture—and to come in with built-in support.

It is also essential to start the process long in advance. Many experts on succession believe the process should start one to three years before succession occurs. Consider setting up metrics, such as 360-degree reviews or performance standards to measure how the new CEO is doing. If the CEO is not working out, it is better to act quickly to find a new CEO than let the problem linger in the usually vain hope things will change.

Do a CEO Survey

Another idea to consider is to run a survey of employees to evaluate the CEO. The NCEO has a sample CEO survey in the documents library in the members area. The survey is designed to assess the CEO's effectiveness in terms of strategy, culture, vision, operations, and structure. In most cases, it would be given to 10-20 people who have regular contact with the CEO, but one company gave it to all employees. The results should be compiled anonymously. Boards should review the findings and either provide the raw tables and comments (making sure to disguise or eliminate anything that would identify someone) or, more commonly, just show the question results and summarize the comments.

In one company that did this, the results from the first survey were disheartening to the CEO. Part of the negative feedback was related to challenges in the company's economic environment, but part was based on what respondents felt was the CEO not being willing to more actively consider and encourage employee ideas. In the ensuing year, the CEO took steps to redress that. The next year's survey showed dramatic improvement, and some of these new ideas helped the bottom line.

Chapter 7, "Governance," discusses CEO surveys in greater detail.

Final Thoughts

Leading an ownership culture company is a challenge—and a joy if you do it right. The easy path is often just to make decisions. After all, if you have risen to that level, you have shown considerable skill and judgment. Creating systems to seek out and encourage more ideas from more people about more things takes a lot of extra time. You have to spend more time in meetings and talking to people. You have to develop the habit of going along with ideas you may think are not very good. You have to be willing to get honest and often difficult feedback.

But if you get this right, you can walk down an office hallway or on a factory floor and hear people having engaged conversations about how to make the business better. You will no longer have subordinates; you will have colleagues. You will lead a company that can be, in business writer John Case's words, an "idea factory." Participating in this community of common purpose is enormously energizing, and you can see that in the evangelical spirit with which these leaders talk about their companies at meetings. It's not easy, but it is well worth doing.

KEY TAKEAWAYS

- Ownership culture companies need to place a priority on hiring and assessing key leaders on how effectively they create and/or enlarge ownership cultures.
- Leadership on any specific issue in an ownership culture should be based more on what you know than where you are in the hierarchy.
- Great ownership culture leaders find ways to instill a sense of shared responsibility. Employee-owners have rights, but they also have obligations.

- Great ownership culture leaders are appropriately humble: they genuinely want to invite and listen to ideas from people at all levels and do not assume their ideas are automatically the best.
- Ownership culture leaders live the company's mission and vision.
- Create a succession plan for multiple levels of the company that puts an emphasis on ownership culture skills. Provide appropriate training for future leaders, and help all employees develop their own career paths.
- Hire CEO successors from within if possible, and get buy-in from employees in the process.
- Consider doing a CEO survey to assess ownership culture and other skills.

CHAPTER 3

Share, Teach, and Use the Numbers

Say you are playing a basketball game, and your team is organized like most companies. Management knows and tracks all the numbers, everything from the overall score to the specific metrics like rebounds, assists, turnovers, etc. They also analyze critical issues, such as in what situations the team does poorly or individuals perform best. But this is secret information—the players don't know any of it, even if they are winning or losing. Now take this one step further and imagine you and your teammates are owners of this team. You still don't get any of this information—it's a secret only management can know and use. But they will implore you as owners to make the numbers better anyway.

Sounds absurd, right? It's not very motivating. Worse, it makes it very difficult to know how to make changes to improve. Yet that is precisely what happens if your employee ownership company does not share, teach, and use the numbers. Any company that wants more ideas from more people about more things needs first to create business literacy and awareness of metrics. Not only does this give people the motivation of playing a game, but it also helps them understand how to evaluate the ideas they generate.

Getting the numbers, both at the corporate and local level (teams, business units, functions such as health care or customer service), provides people with an ongoing way to assess what they are doing and identify potential weaknesses and opportunities. A common concern about encouraging more employee ideas is that they will be impractical. Maybe they cost too much money, or really would not be worth the investment relative to other things a company could be doing. Or they might push up one good number, say increasing quality, at the expense of pushing down another, such as the number of units produced per day. When business owners think about the numbers, they think about how all the numbers at each level interact with one another to impact growth, profit, and stock value. If employees are owners, they need to learn to think this way too.

Sharing the numbers can also help employees focus their new ideas not just on improving the annual picnic or providing more leave time—ideas that often come up when employees are asked in a vacuum about how to improve work—but on the issues that really matter for company performance. They can't do that if they do not know what the issues are.

It may seem like a daunting task, but many employee ownership companies have shown that it's not only possible, but even fun. Lots of people like tracking numbers, whether they are detailed sports statistics, political polls, their 401(k) account, their steps or carbs per day, their gas mileage, and on and on. These numbers may be related to a personal goal or they may just be for fun. To assume employees cannot learn and use business numbers is a naïve and dangerous misstep.

But sharing the numbers is not enough. It's great to see the year-end financials or how your team is doing against its goals of, say, improving on-time delivery. That may provide more of a sense of ownership, but unless employees have structured opportunities to discuss the numbers and come up with ideas they are empowered to implement, sharing the numbers just ends up being a symbolic exercise.

Getting Started: Share the Why

Steve Baker is the vice president and Rich Armstrong the president of the Great Game of Business, the consulting firm that ESOP-owned SRC Holdings created to help teach other companies how their open-book management system works. SRC may be the most successful ESOP ever—its open-book story will be detailed later in this chapter. In their 2019 book *Get in the Game,* Baker and Armstrong note that implementing the kinds of changes described here can be difficult: "Too often companies jump right into how the change will happen rather than first communicating why the change is important. Simply put, people get much more excited about the How when they clearly understand the Why."

It should seem easy in an ESOP company to get people to know "why." After all, their financial futures are at stake, and it may seem too obvious to bother mentioning that improved profitability leads (all else equal!) to higher stock value. But just knowing that the company's stock price is related to their financial security is not enough. You are now asking people to learn new skills, both in understanding and in using the numbers. There will be managers and supervisors who think having workers take the time to do this takes them away from their real work. There will be line employees who will react with a dazed expression saying they are bored, confused, or both.

We like to convey a sense of excitement: that the numbers tell a fascinating story, full of plot twists, cliff-hangers, courage, outside forces, determination, quick reactions, failures, and successes. On top of that, all of these are about the health of the company of which we are all collectively stewards.

So leaders need to tell a compelling story about the change. Key points to include are:

- Employee-owners have the need to know the numbers, good and bad.
- Employee-owners also have the *responsibility* to know and use the numbers. Following the numbers is the only way to measure if what you and your team are doing or considering doing works.
- The numbers may seem complex or boring, but they are the score, and keeping score in any game is more interesting than not.
- Show how the numbers relate to profits and profits relate to share price.
- Make it a story: who cares that inventory-days are down to 86? But it's great if Frank noticed that BigCo just opened a new location and used that as an occasion to send a note of congratulations that also happened to mention their overdue invoice.

- Make it personal—share why you decided to do this and how you hope this can help transform the company.
- Consider inviting an employee-owner from another company that does this to tell their story.

The most compelling why, of course, is how the numbers relate to profits and profits to share price. Most employees don't know much about what profits are, much less how they drive share value. Many employees confuse profits with sales, or assume that profits are a high percentage of sales (often more than 50%). Some exercises can help with this (and these should be done regularly for new employees and any current employees who want a refresher).

Stock Value: The Ultimate Why

As an owner, the big payoff is what your stock is worth. But valuation seems like a complex black box. You need to make it real.

There are several steps in making this happen:

- *Outline the concepts and methods.* The details and complexities of income-based methods and market-based methods of valuation can be overwhelming, but the basic concepts aren't difficult. One ESOP company used a slide show to announce a new valuation that explained the income approach as "how well are we performing" and the market approach as "how we compare to similar but publicly traded companies." Another way to make these concepts accessible is by using the home appraisal analogy. An appraiser would look at what comparable homes are selling for in the same neighborhood and estimate the value of the home based on future rental income.
- *Annually explain the basic idea behind valuation explored in the Harry the Horse Game (below).* The most important concept for employees and work groups to understand is the power of the multiple as it applies to your company's earnings. The power of the multiple is huge. When employees understand that a buyer or

The Profit Exercise

Have everyone gather and tell them your total sales. Now divide them into small groups (4-10 people) and have them discuss how much of sales are profits. Ask them to outline the costs that reduce the sales number to the profits number and make some guesses about these. Their guesses may be wildly off, but that is not the point. The exercise gets them thinking about the issue.

Now have everyone reconvene and each group can report its profits number. Ask each group to also list one cost and its guess for that.

Now have the CFO or CEO show the real numbers. You don't need to display a 50-item income statement. Just hit the basics (salary, rent, utilities, marketing expense, benefits, depreciation (which you need to explain), taxes, etc.). Take one item at a time and subtract it. Some companies go even further and take a dollar bill and cut it into smaller and smaller pieces (this is illegal, by the way, so consider a replica). If you want to be really creative, give one to every small group and let them cut up their own bills as part of the discussion process.

The resulting number will, of course, be pretty small relative to sales. Now ask people how much they would have to increase sales for another $10,000 in profit—or how much they would have to reduce costs. It makes the $100 you save here and there seem a lot more meaningful.

investor will pay a much greater amount for a company's annual earnings than the company will generate in the next few years, they can begin to understand how their small ideas and positive actions influence stock value. People should understand that, all else being equal, every dollar a company's earnings goes up causes a several-dollar increase in the value of its stock. If the multiple is 5 to 1, then an idea that saves or earns the company an extra $1,000 a year is actually worth $5,000 in value. Ten ideas that increase earnings by $1,000 actually create another $50,000 in value. People should also know that the opposite is true when the company loses money. A decrease in earnings is also multiplied! This is a very powerful concept for engaged employees to understand, and it helps illustrate how their decisions and many small ideas can maximize share value.

- *Bring it on home.* Try using excerpts from an actual valuation report to communicate these concepts more clearly. Show employees the ratios that the valuators used and the effect increasing profit or paying off debt had on stock value. Concrete numbers from your own company are more readily understood and used by employee-owners.

A lot of ESOP companies break employees into small groups before the report is presented and ask them to guess the new value. The idea here is to get people to think about this beforehand so when the number is presented, they are more ready to learn.

The Harry the Horse Exercise

Profits are great, of course, and maybe in your company they also trigger some incentive pay. But the real payoff of being an owner is this: in a conventional company with profit sharing, if you generate another $100,000 in profits, maybe the employees get $10,000 to share. But the owners of the remaining $90,000 get a multiple of that (usually 3-7 times) in share value if the savings will be replicable year after year. So the key point of ownership is simple:

> *As a profit sharer, you get a percentage of the added profits you help create. As an owner, you get a multiple.*

So how can you make this power of the multiple more real to people? For many years, we been have doing this with the Harry the Horse game. Here is how it works:

Harry the Horse: The ESOP Valuation Game

This game is meant to help employees understand how valuation is tied to profits. It takes about 30 to 45 minutes depending on the size of the group, or 20 if you are in a hurry and do an abbreviated version.

The moderator first has people divide into tables of six to eight people. They are told that Harry is a horse whose owner wants to sell him. Half of the table owns Harry the Horse and wants to sell him. The other half is considering buying Harry. Harry is three years old. Most colts who are successful can race about another five years and then can be put out to stud for many more years. Harry is in good health. In the last year, Harry won $300,000 in prizes; the labor, stabling, food, transportation, insurance, and other costs for owning him are $250,000. Sellers meet for 5 to 10 minutes to come up with an asking price. Buyers do the same to decide what to pay. Then they take 5 to 10 more minutes to negotiate.

After they negotiate, a reporter from each table reports what price the buyers and sellers agreed on. In some cases, the buyers and sellers cannot reach an agreement. In that case, the reporter should say what the buyers were willing to bid and what the sellers were willing to pay. Then the moderator asks the whole group what factors they considered.

The moderator needs to make sure at least the following factors come up and are explained:

- Risks (health, better competition, race track closings)
- How else an investor could use the money to buy Harry and how much would the investor make by doing it?
- How risky is Harry is relative to other investments?
- What is the rate of return a buyer wants from owning Harry?
- What are general economic conditions? Interest rates? Attitudes toward stocks in general?
- How easily can the investor get cash for Harry if he or she wants to sell relative to other kinds of investment?

The moderator then explains that an investor looks at Harry by figuring out what kind of annual rate of return he or she wants given how risky the investment is and what else could be invested in. Explain how different kinds of investments (CDs, mutual funds, real estate, stock in a public company, or an individual company) vary in risk and required return. The table below has some rates for 2019, listed by the ascending level of risk:

CDs	<1% to 2%
Government bonds	1.5% to 2.5%
Investment grade corporate bonds	3% to 5%
High-yield (risk) corporate bonds	6% to 8%
Historical average for mutual funds	8% to 10%
Private equity investments (generally in a limited number of companies)	14% to 21%

We suggest you put these investments on a chart without the numbers and ask people to tell you what they think the rates are. You may need to explain some of these investments.

Explain how some investments are worth more because they are easier to cash in, allowing you to use the money for other investment opportunities that come up. Explain that higher interest rates mean lower stock values, other things being equal, because if rates are higher, it is more tempting not to take risks. And explain that a shaky economy drives down all stock values because people don't want to invest.

The table results can now be expressed by the moderator as a yearly rate of return. If Harry made $50,000 in profits and a buyer will pay $200,000, then that buyer wants a 25% rate of return (i.e., a price-to-earnings multiple of 4) if it is assumed Harry will earn $50,000 a year for the next four years. I.e., from an initial investment of $200,000, each year the buyer would receive 25% ($50,000) in profit. But there are other factors too. If Harry's earnings are likely to go up each year, the buyer can pay more and get the same rate of return (show why). Also, Harry has some residual asset value. Alas, if Harry dies, then maybe it is only for glue, but if Harry has had a successful career, and can be put out to stud, then that generates an income stream over a longer period of time—and people will pay for that.

It is not essential to come up with a precise multiple, although we recommend you use and discuss the multiple in your company. The point is that Harry is like your company—a riskier investment than some other things, but still one that people will pay some multiple of earnings to buy.

So now point out that if employees can generate another $100,000 in profits, if they were in a profit-sharing company they would get maybe $10,000 or $15,000 of that. In most companies, they would get nothing at all, of course, because there is no profit sharing. The owner, meanwhile, gets a multiple (you can use 5 as a typical multiple) of the earnings that have been added, if they can create year-to-year savings. So if $90,000 is left after profit sharing, the owner's equity goes up $450,000! If the employees are owners, that is their money. Employee-owners, then, get a multiple of the earnings they create; employee profit sharers get a percentage. Of course, they also get a multiple of losses, but in a market economy, it is risk that creates reward.

It will take time in most companies for most people to see the why—although some will get it right away and be enthused—but the almost universal experience in ESOPs is that people do learn why and come to genuinely appreciate that working at a company that does this really sets their experience apart.

What Numbers to Share

There are two sets of numbers to share. The first are overall corporate numbers—the income statement, balance sheet, and cash flow. There is usually not much point in sharing a detailed multi-page statement. It's too much information to absorb and far too much to use. But companies can and should share the highlights, explain how they work, show how they varied from prior years and the budget, and highlight the more detailed numbers where there was a substantial variance.

This level of information sharing has great symbolic value, but the payoff comes from developing and using metrics at the work level and linking them to the top line. These metrics are the critical numbers in each work group—quality, output, cost per unit, absorption rates, returns, customer retention, and many more—that each group can use and have some control over. Some companies post these numbers daily in work areas, but most use some subset of them at team meetings. Some companies build incentives around meeting targets for these numbers in individual groups.

The last step is to link these local numbers to the big picture. First, your communications team should work on identifying the "critical numbers" at your company. For example, employee-owners need to know how their jobs connect to their departments' goals, how their departments contribute to the health of the company, how company performance changes the stock price, and how the stock price affects the value of employee accounts. Your team might use some or all of these or come up with your own, but it's important that these concepts can be measured and communicated clearly. Critical numbers are both the company-wide and team-based numbers that drive performance. Similarly, you need to assess critical weaknesses—numbers that need improving. Red Dot Corporation, an ESOP-owned manufacturing company in Washington, places a chart of metrics outside each work area that is regularly updated in colored text so that the teams can track progress. (Red Dot also places big hanging banners in the plant with names of retired employees and how much they got in the ESOP.)

Start by picking the most important critical numbers at your company by organizing a group of employees that represents the whole workforce, including middle management and executives. Have the group brainstorm the answers to this question: "What do people need to understand to be effective employee-owners at this company?" Use a white board or sticky notes to keep track of each and focus on generating lots of ideas. Once all possible concepts have been gathered, you can consolidate similar ideas into groups and remove those that just don't fit.

Baker and Armstrong describe the process in detail. They suggest an employee survey ask these questions:

- What does the company do well?
- What doesn't the company do well?
- What are the critical "financial" issues facing the company in the next six to twelve months?
- What are the critical "marketplace or customer" issues facing the company in the next six to twelve months?
- What are the critical "operational or process" issues facing the company in the next six to twelve months?
- What are the critical "people or cultural" issues facing the company in the next six to twelve months?
- What is "one thing" we can achieve in the next six to twelve months that would have the greatest impact on the overall performance of the business?

With the results of the survey and the initial meetings, SRC critical numbers design teams, usually made up of key managers both for the company overall and site by site joined with selected people from the nonmanagement employees, meet to create the critical numbers for each location and overall. The teams will review input from management about what issues are not covered, as well as look at issues the employees raised that management did not, with the goal of finding the numbers that work for the company and the employees. Note that once a critical number target is met, it may be time to move on to other ones as an area of focus.

In their book Baker and Armstrong say that to assess critical numbers, ask:

- Does the company have (or can it get) the resources, skills, time, and support needed to achieve the Critical Number?

- Is the Critical Number impactful?
- Financial impact: Will the Critical Number keep people focused on the fundamentals of business: making money and generating cash?
- Strategic impact: Will the Critical Number make the company stronger and healthier, by eliminating our weaknesses and growing strategically?
- Educational impact: Will the Critical Number help educate people about the different aspects of the business and teach people exactly what it takes to be successful?
- Is the Critical Number timely? Does it represent something that needs to be done now, or are there other things that need to be done first? Does it need to be done quickly, before things get worse or the window closes?

When goals are met, celebrate. Let others know that a team achieved a critical number and how they did it. Have a company-wide event if you meet company numbers.

You can use the same building blocks for any critical numbers your team comes up with on a more localized, task specific level. These critical numbers apply only to that issue. Say one key concept is reducing shipping errors. First, have the shipping team define what is meant by this. An error might mean shipping the wrong product to a customer. This means that your company not only needs to cover the cost of shipping the correct item a second time but also needs to expedite it to satisfy your customer. Multiple errors can be very costly and start to add up. Have your design team show how shipping errors are tracked and measured. Then explain the relationship between your company's shipping errors and its earnings each year. Now ask employees to generate ideas on reducing shipping errors. Finish with a report on what ideas will be pursued and what impact they might have on your company's overall performance as you track these improvements over the course of the year.

As this example shows, critical numbers include both overall company goals and more specific drivers in various parts of your business.

You want to focus on the sweet spot numbers that have a significant impact and for which the needed skills and resources either exist or are worth the time to develop.

Developing localized numbers like shipping errors essentially replicates the company-wide critical number process. One good way to work on these numbers is "mini-games," a powerful concept pioneered by SRC. Have the employees in the affected area form a team (if they have not already) to help specifically define the problem and the goal in measurable, achievable terms. Determine what resources are needed and if the problem's solution will merit the cost. If so, set a time frame to achieve the goal and measure results along the way. Let the team choose its own rewards, within some budget you provide. You might want to limit the rewards to non-cash items—cash is quickly spent and the reward is not large enough to be memorable. Instead, let the team pick from fun things to do, like meals, tickets to games or events, a charitable contribution, etc.

Baker and Armstrong say the key attributes of mini-games are:

- Establishes line of sight.
- Everyone has a chance to win.
- Rules are clear and simple.
- Easily measured and scored with a simple scoreboard.
- Frequent scoring for constant reinforcement.
- Competition against a problem or opportunity, not each other.
- Scoring rewards positive outcomes, not competition.
- Limited duration, or early first round winners.
- Rewards encourage participation, not competition.
- Prizes reward performance, not motivate performance.
- Goal is meaningful to the team's overall performance.
- Scorekeeper settles disputes.
- Incorporates business training to aid understanding.

- Promotes long-term change.
- Doesn't cause problems for other work groups or departments.

SRC: The Ultimate Case of Using and Sharing the Numbers

No company exemplifies the idea of sharing and using the numbers more than SRC. Its CEO, Jack Stack, literally wrote the book on the subject, and no company has had more influence, in part through its subsidiary, The Great Game of Business, on how people think about this.

In 1983, Springfield ReManufacturing Company (now SRC Holdings) was a failing division of International Harvester. It had $16 million in sales, 116 employees, one business unit, and its stock was worth 10 cents. Thirteen of its managers used their own money and a lot of debt to buy the company, and then set up a 31% ESOP to share the hoped-for gains.

Today, SRC is 100% ESOP-owned, with 1,790 employees, over $600 million in sales, and 12 business units, and its most recent (2018) valuation was well over $760 per share.

It wasn't magic. SRC grew because Jack Stack, its CEO then and now, made the seemingly radical decision to teach every employee the financial and operational details of the company and have them meet weekly in small huddles to make decisions about using these numbers to help the company grow. Stack called his idea "The Great Game of Business," which also became the title of a best-selling book by him and Bo Burlingham.

Because SRC has done this so well for so long, its story deserves to serve as a template. What follows in this section is based on a presentation by Steve Baker at the 2017 NCEO annual conference.

Start with the Overall Common Sense Financials

Employees won't learn much from nor be able to use a detailed company financial statement. So SRC focuses on what is called common sense financials. These are simplified versions of standard financial statements that revolve around the company's critical numbers. SRC focuses on usable numbers, not accounting. Bakers says this "includes understanding how profitability is driven, how assets are used, how cash is generated, but most importantly how employees' day-to-day actions and decisions impact business success. Employees rarely need to know about debits and credits or how to do an adjusting entry. But, depending on the company, they may very well need to know exactly how production efficiency is calculated, or why receivable days matter, or how the purchase of a new computer system will affect the income statement and balance sheet. The bottom line is this: People remember what they find relevant and useful." These numbers are then discussed within the broader corporate strategic context.

The numbers are for the whole company but are also unbundled by business units and work teams. SRC creates these numbers through a bottom-up process. Every employee is involved in weekly huddles to look at their critical numbers, as well to modify and develop them in the first place. A key goal is understanding that the numbers are not just what you have done, but what you expect to do, so are driving the company looking forward, not backward. While management still plays its usual role in developing financials and creating budgets, Baker says "front line employees are responsible for tracking, measuring, and reporting their own operational numbers as well as how those numbers impact financial results. These employees are responsible for helping to gather the data that goes into their line items, reporting their numbers to the company, and for understanding what's happening to their line items over time."

The numbers come more alive at SRC by focusing on a few key concepts:

- Variances ("red flag" management)
- Benchmarking
- Trends
- All-time records
- Relationships (with other numbers)

- Line of sight
- Stories (both successes and failures)
- Forecasting (cause and effect)

While all the relevant numbers are discussed in the huddles, with ownership of various line items assigned to individuals, the key focus is on the one or more critical numbers the team has identified. Goals are set for how to improve those numbers, and often "mini-games" are created to get employees together to figure out how to achieve the goal. Once the goal is achieved, the group often moves on to new critical weaknesses to resolve because the old ones now are not an issue anymore.

This process takes a lot of time, time that may seem better spent on "working." But Stack would insist this is the most important work people do.

MSA

While SRC has the best-elaborated system, elements of this idea show up in lots of other ways. For some companies, the full-fledged Great Game doesn't work, and they just use pieces. Others take their own approaches.

MSA is a 330-employee company organized by market types, serving municipal, transportation, and developer clients with civil engineering, planning, surveying, architecture, environmental science, and geographic information services. It has offices in Wisconsin, Minnesota, Iowa, Illinois, Georgia, and Texas. MSA became a partial ESOP in 1991 and became a 100% ESOP S corp in 2017. MSA started with the Great Game of Business in the late 1990s. Although the game aspect never really stuck for MSA, many of the innovations of the Great Game have been folded into MSA's culture, including huddling, open book management, monthly forecasts, and financial literacy.

The MSA approach now includes:

- Monthly one-on-one check-ins between supervisor and employee
- Monthly team, office, or program huddles

- Quarterly all-company updates
- Financial literacy training
- Goal-setting at the team level, and
- An annual incentive plan based on company, team, and individual performance.

The implementation of the Great Game system led MSA to establish a monthly scorecard of critical numbers. At MSA, the critical number is gross profit from operations, which is easy to display on a monthly basis, track over time, and measure against the financial plan. Other critical key performance indicators include wage utilization, backlog (work under contract but not performed), pipeline (work that the company is aware of, prorated based on the likelihood of our capturing it), days unbilled and receivable, and net multiplier and revenue factor, which is the ratio of revenue produced to wage expense. In the engineering and architecture business, wages are far and away the largest expense, so this ratio is a very good indicator of a team's ability to monetize the time of their staff. On the team level, the key performance metric is the revenue factor, which accounts for both utilization and multiplier.

Financial literacy is a key aspect of new employee orientation, and is also featured in the quarterly updates, annual meetings, and training for project managers. The company's controller discusses the numbers and what they mean for the coming periods. Financial information is shared monthly with all supervisory staff, and they are encouraged to share it at their team huddles. In addition, the information is posted to the company's intranet, Mosaic. Single issue financial charts track other key numbers, such as backlog, utilization, billing/cash collection ratio, and marketing efforts.

Each month, the leadership team of MSA convenes for an eight-hour meeting to go over all current operational topics, financial projections, and performance. Each of the shared services departments (accounting, HR, IT, marketing and client services) provides an update, with the goal being that all members of the leadership team are knowledgeable of any new issues and can effectively communicate them down their chain of command. Each month, a guest is chosen to attend the meeting so that others can gain an understanding of what the leadership team is addressing. In addition, a member of the 35-and-under group will typically attend the full meeting and give an update on what their young professional cohort is engaged in.

Team leaders are expected to meet with their employees at monthly huddles to review key numbers and indicators, such as hourly utilization, backlog, gross profits from operations, work in progress, new projects, sales, and bonus funding. Scorecards help visually track performance on all these measures. Teams usually meet at breakfast or lunch to review progress and ideas. Because of the nature of the company's work, however, it can be difficult to get everyone together at the same time. The concentration on key numbers makes it simple to break down complex financial topics. The measurements provide an incentive to perform in themselves—everyone likes to win the game, even if there aren't rewards (but rewards make it much more interesting). They also help employees focus their ideas on those issues that are most important to driving company success.

This focus on the key numbers allowed the company to remain profitable through the great recession. A combination of top-line revenue growth and improvement in the bottom line has allowed the company's profit to grow by a factor of seven since the low point in 2012. In addition, the company has put a greater emphasis on rebuilding the health of the organization by increasing investments in training and development, upgrading office spaces, leadership development, building 16 internal communities of practice, implementing a quality initiative, and other improvement efforts. These, coupled with a consistent focus on the critical numbers, will allow MSA to remain a vibrant, independent business.

Short Takes from Other Companies

Pacific Outdoor Living

Pacific Outdoor Living is a leading Southern California outdoor living and landscape design and construction firm. It set up its ESOP in 2017. That fit well in an existing open book, high involvement culture. As part of that, Terry Morrill, the CEO, developed a booklet called "Am I Making Money?" It is an easy to read, illustrated guide for all employees, with clever cartoon-like characters. The book walks employees through understanding how much projects are making and what the various components are.

That is the static part. The interactive part is a software system everyone can access. It is essentially a job status board that looks at each project, how it is progressing, who is responsible for each phase, etc. Employees can track material delays, labor hours, labor days, wages paid, gross product and gross product margins, commissions, and sales price. Estimating and scheduling software are also used. From these, employees can track whether projects are making money or not. The schedule board and job management system totals the gross profit made at the end of each day, so there is no more waiting for monthly or quarterly reports. If the hours involved are more than what is needed to hit targets, teams can talk about ways to solve the problem. The system has worked so well that they now do coaching with other contractors wanting to see how it is done.

Barclay Water Management

This 100% ESOP-owned company we discussed earlier has more than half its employees in the field on any day selling Barclay's products. Most of its contracts are for a fixed price and term.

For many years, Barclay paid its sales staff incentives based on total sales. But soon after its transition to an ESOP, it started to pay based on contributions to overhead and profit. Under the prior system, salespeople had an incentive to do whatever was needed to make the customer happy, such as delivering a resupply overnight or providing an additional service at no cost. Under the new system that would reduce incentive pay.

To make this work better, an engineer at Barclay developed an internal software system that every salesperson could use and update on a real-time basis. As any modification was made, the salesperson would immediately see the impact on overhead and profit—and so could all the other salespeople. Salespeople are competitive and started looking at just how well their peers were doing and, even better, trading ideas on what contract changes they could charge for or provide differently without losing customers.

This system operates within a larger structure of a long history of sharing financials with employees quarterly through a newsletter and president's discussion, as well as a detailed discussion at the annual meeting.

Van Meter

Van Meter Inc. is a 100% ESOP-owned wholesale and electrical supplier in rural Iowa. After building a base level of ESOP understanding for its employee-owners, its ESOP committee saw the next step as finding ways for each employee to contribute to increasing the stock price. To do that, employee-owners need to understand something about valuation. The committee quickly realized that valuation analysis is long and complicated, so they looked for a way to translate the factors that drive value into easy-to-use terms. The result is the "your two cents worth" campaign, which the committee launched in 2005. Based on current numbers and some simplifying assumptions, the campaign is built on a simple formula: improving VMI's bottom line by $5,000 creates an expected increase of $0.02 in the value of a VMI share. This equation doesn't capture the complexity of the actual valuation process, but it does close the loop between each employee and the value of the company. It also makes for easy math to show what happens to the value of the stock if all employees do their own two cents worth, something that the ESOP committee emphasizes in monthly updates about operational improvements.

CMC Rescue

CMC Rescue is a manufacturer of specialized equipment for high-risk rescue environments, such as fire, search and rescue, swift water, air operations, and more. The company is owned by its ESOP.

One of the ways its shares numbers is through its line of sight program. Each employee has a chart with a graphic that links individual to department to company performance. The individual's line of site is a specific set of metrics and commitments each employee makes, with a heading of "How My Contributions Affect CMC Rescue's Performance." They are all posted on a common site. For instance, a planner and scheduler's included:

- Improving on-time delivery percentage.
- Providing the right due date to the right team.
- Identifying if orders are late and letting customers know.
- Communicating priorities to shipping, manufacturing, and warehouse to make sure everyone is on the same team.
- Providing accurate information to those who need to know about scheduling issues.

By linking these objectives to specific numbers in a cascading way, from the individual to the team to the company's overall profitability and sales goals, everyone makes commitments to what they can do to move the company forward.

CMC's Beth Henry says to make this work effectively, the company runs workshops on the line of sight issue. The workshop objectives are to:

- Understand the importance of employees' roles in the organization
- Explore the company's mission, vision, and values
- Connect employee contributions to the company's success
- Share company results proudly and openly

Workshops are organized into groups of 10 to 12, with one manager and one facilitator. Henry says the leaders should be ready to get the process rolling, helping brainstorm and dialog openly, and connecting the dots between what they do and how the company makes money. Employees then complete a one-page worksheet illustrating their unique contributions (not their job duties) and how they impact department and, ultimately, company success. Facilitators must be comfortable discussing the basics of financial performance and how it drives ESOP share value.

These quick takes provide a variety of more granular ideas on elements of an open-book system. In each company, they are part of a larger process. In your own company, enlist your ESOP committee to help come up with ideas, working with the CFO and teams leaders to identify which numbers to share and what to do with them.

It's Not Just the Money

Finally, companies should not frame sharing and using the numbers solely in terms of people's monetary self-interest. It's tempting to do that, but "WIIFM" is not a sufficient framework. People need to know that when employees have ideas that improve the bottom line, they are creating value for all of their coworkers too. Employee-owners are motivated by the sense of community that employee ownership can provide. Making the lives of their colleagues better is a powerful motivator. In fact, in general, people are motivated less at work by calculations of rational economic return than by, as author Daniel Pink says in *Drive*, having a sense of purpose, autonomy, and mastery. Sharing and using the numbers can make that happen.

KEY TAKEAWAYS

- Not sharing the numbers is like playing a game and not knowing the score.
- The overall company numbers are mostly symbolic in value; the key drivers are at the team and business unit levels.
- Relate the why of number sharing, both in how they drive profits and how profits affect the power of the multiple in share price.
- The numbers are not just financial but all the key metrics that drive performance.
- Employees need to be involved in determining what numbers matter most so they own the process.

- Consider short-term incentives for finding ways to improve the numbers.
- The process is iterative—you will try some things and find some work and some don't. You'll get better over time.
- Celebrate wins.

CHAPTER 4

How to Create an Ideas Generation Process

Teaching employees how to understand and use the numbers is a critical first step in creating high involvement cultures. But it's not enough to get where you need to be. Employees need to be able to use that information to generate and implement ideas. Listen to what CEO Nick Palmer of Commercial Casework has to say about this.

Commercial Casework Inc. is a 100% ESOP-owned provider of custom commercial woodwork for premier companies throughout the San Francisco Bay Area. It has been practicing open book management for nearly 25 years and has been a regular presenter at Great Game of Business conferences. It all started when Bill Palmer, Commercial Casework's founder (and father of current CEO Nick Palmer) read *The Great Game of Business*. The company became a leading Great Game player, sharing both broad corporate financials and metrics for each operation and project. While that helped the company succeed, by 2018 Nick Palmer realized it was not enough.

Palmer told us that to move forward, "we had to start changing the ways we incorporate employees in our decision making, thus gaining a higher level of engagement. First, all new employees are required to read *The Great Game of Business*, followed by four or five group meetings of up to 10 employees with a senior leader to discuss the chapters and how they relate to Commercial Casework Inc. This is the first opportunity/exposure that employees have to the financials." It is an essential first step because new employees have not had exposure to reading and using financials. That helps them understand how the company works and make better sense of the weekly companywide meetings held to discuss the current "State of Commercial Casework Inc."

In 2018, Commercial Casework added a secondary class for all employees to dive into the financials on a much more detailed level. Again, these are groups of up to 10 employees. Aside from discussing the financials, they make clear to the employee(s) that this is an opportunity to ask any question regarding the numbers. For employees who are usually out in the field, the company also offers a quarterly review prior to the general update.

All of that is just preparation. Having more financially educated employees is great, but Palmer says the key is to take the next step and get people to use this information to improve company operations, not just by making more effort but by contributing more ideas.

"Leading from the top down doesn't work," Palmer says. "You need to get lower level employees excited about change. We have started a yearly (possibly quarterly in 2019) SWOT (strengths, weaknesses, opportunities, and threats) meeting that is a blend of senior managers as well as up-and-coming employees who may very well replace managers as retirements come up. This is an opportunity for lower level employees to contribute their ideas and get a stronger understanding of where the company is headed. Employees like to talk to other employees; they don't want to hear change from a manager or the CEO. If you can get employees excited about change, it spreads like wildfire."

The company uses its lean manufacturing as a lead-in for people to take time to review how work processes can be refined. The company creates regular opportunities for employees to get together to talk about these ideas and figure out how to implement them.

Palmer says that all of this is just what he hopes to be the start of a developing process to use the financial literacy that the company has worked hard to build with people into structured, regular opportunities for employees to meet and discuss what can be done to improve operation and the work experience of Commercial Casework at all levels.

Commercial Casework is just starting its journey to finding ways to generate more ideas from more people. They have set their own path to that, but what is the best way to set yours?

Management could set up a process, or it could hire outside consultants to develop one. If done well, the result could be an efficient, elegant approach imposed from the top down. Chances are, though, that an imposed system will not get enough buy-in from enough people to work. A company might also hire a consulting firm that has experience with employee involvement in employee ownership companies. There are now a handful of these, and while their specific approaches differ, all approach the task as a collaborative effort, working with leadership and employees to develop a system that works for them and has their input in its creation.

While outside help can be very beneficial in guiding your decisions, many companies develop their own processes internally. To do that, companies start by having people read key books on employee involvement (see our brief suggested reading list at the end), sending a team to ESOP conferences to attend panels on employee involvement, and visiting nearby companies that are experienced in employee involvement. The ESOP community is remarkable willing to share its experience. Harpoon Brewing, for instance, sent people to learn from Web; now people come to visit Harpoon.

The employee team doing this homework should come back with a list of ideas that seem worth trying, but understand that finding the right approach usually has potholes and false starts. Where you start does not have to be where you end. The key is to start somewhere, evaluate progress, make changes, rinse, and repeat.

In getting started, be careful not to let your ambitions exceed your grasp. Maybe you went to an NCEO conference or visited a mature company like some of those profiled in this book and decided "let's do that." But "that" may be a bridge too far for many companies. If you have never had an ideas process before beyond a suggestion box or open doors, the kind of elaborate system you'll see described below may be such a dramatic change that it won't do what you hope.

Consider the key lessons in *Ideas Are Free* about why these systems can fail:

- *Idea Initiatives Are Strictly Top-Down:* In a typical workplace, it is simply impossible for managers to be completely aware of all the problems or opportunities for improvement in the business, whereas employees on the frontlines can identify far more of these in their day-to-day work than top-down management ever could. This is why authors Schroeder and Robinson put a great deal of focus on practices that encourage much greater attention to everyday issues. While it may make a lot of sense for management to focus on big-picture strategic thinking, your company should consider all the value that small ideas from every employee can create.
- *The Process for Submitting Ideas Is Too Ambiguous:* We have rarely been introduced to a company that does not have an open-door policy, but when it comes to maximizing the insights and experiences from all employees, as we noted in chapter one, giving them permission to walk through the boss's door simply isn't enough. Ideas should not only be encouraged and welcome, but the process for submitting them should be clear and simple as well. A large majority of the ideas coming from employees are fairly modest and easy to implement. This means that they really should not require large forms to fill out and a series of managers to review them before they can be implemented. At ESOP-owned Carris Reels, idea boards include 3-by-5 cards. The cards include descriptions of small ideas that can be implemented almost immediately by employees and management on the shop floor to improve safety or efficiency. This both saves time and enables employees to implement ideas on their own without much need for management's approval. More complex ideas can be further assessed by a more elaborate processes.
- *Evaluation of Ideas Is Time-Consuming and Ineffective:* Take the storied suggestion box (maybe now it exists on your website). Sure, the submission of an idea to a suggestion box may be pretty straightforward and simple, but what happens next? If you are en-

couraging multiple small ideas from every employee, the workload and time needed to evaluate the ideas can add up quickly. The person evaluating the ideas may not be the right one, and the process for moving forward is usually unclear. Maybe that is why one wag said "any company that uses a suggestion box to gets suggestions needs suggestions about how to get suggestions." Decision making around ideas should really be in the hands of those most familiar with the situation: the employees. Rather than create a system that constantly requires ideas to go up a chain of command, create a structure—weekly department level meetings, for example—where decisions can be made on the spot, or as close as possible.

- *Failure to Recognize and Celebrate Employee Ideas:* Recognition and reward can be tricky, controversial even, but according to Schroeder and Robinson, the most effective form of recognition for employee ideas is to actually use them. People take pride in contributing to the company's success. As Jack Stack says, "People support what they help create," and sometimes the most effective reward is acknowledgement—giving credit where credit is due—and a big "thank you." Some companies have annual events to recognize employees for their involvement in the ideas system; others post good ideas in their newsletter or a regular email; others provide small rewards; and some even give awards at random just for submitting an idea.

It is also important to be very clear about boundaries. In each company, what you are comfortable with having employees decide will vary. It may start on just a few issues, or be limited to projects with under a certain cost, for instance. Often, these will expand over time. Employees may, however, wonder why if they are owners they cannot make more decisions about more things. This is especially problematic if you have not defined what they can decide and what they can only have input on. For at least some people, expectations will exceed reality, and lead to cynicism.

Chris Mackin of Ownership Associates, a Cambridge consulting firm, has developed an especially useful framework for thinking about this, which he calls Frontiers and Boundaries. Mackin says that:

"The idea of employee ownership is provocative. Few people can think about becoming joint owners of their workplace without expecting things to change, often in fundamental ways. For some people, employee ownership is part of a rational, just, and participatory way of doing business. For others, it risks the unparalleled chaos of everyone being involved in every decision, with no one left to attend to business."

"Companies have a basic choice when faced with these expectations. They can, within the framework of most corporate and ERISA law, ignore or even actively deny them. A few companies have reflexively attempted to fully satisfy all possible expectations and create an ideal direct democracy in the workplace. A third alternative...is that companies can listen, engage and work with employee expectations by transparently mapping how decision-making can be shared—without giving up the right to manage...People can and should be involved in many different aspects of the company, but it shouldn't be in an unclear, fuzzy, or "boundary-less" way."

Mackin has developed his own training program around this idea, but companies can also try to develop their own approaches by having management and the ideas team meet to map out which decisions can be made at which levels. In some cases, employees will have no role; in others input; and still others, they can make decisions on their own.

Table 4-1 provides a detailed map of the decisions and the level of input to consider.

Table 4-1. Participation checklist

Work issue	Decides alone	Formally recommends to management	Has input only	Who is on team?
Human resources				
Hiring, firing, or career development				
Selection or review of supervisors/management				
Work rules, vacation, benefits, compensation				
Complaint resolution procedures				
Worker training and evaluation				

Table 4-1. Participation checklist

Work issue	Decides alone	Formally recommends to management	Has input only	Who is on team?
Overseeing participation process				
Working conditions and work design				
Product and service development				
Process change				
Process evaluation				
Customer service response				
Process and/or quality control				
Work space layout and design				
Supplier relations				
Just-in-time or lean management				
Supplier quality assessment and improvement				
Selection of equipment				
Material tracking and use				
Customer relations				
New customer development				
Customer service response and measurement				
Billing, collection, and contracts				
Corporate issues				
Strategic issues				
Product/service development				
Corporate finance training				
Developing and using critical numbers				
Mission/value statements				
Information flows other than finance				
Marketing				
Safety				
Social events				
Healthcare/wellness programs				

This is just a basic schematic. In your company, you can define the issues more specifically. "Input" should be defined as well. Most important, you need to explain to people why these roles are what they are. Over time, you may find that you will want to change these roles, such as involving employees more in strategic decisions, as described in a later chapter.

In this chapter, we'll look at systems for getting employees started. Some are very simple; some more elaborate. They are all just suggestions of places to start, but get employee input and find your own. The next chapter will delve more into details about employee teams making decisions about work-level issues, followed by a chapter on getting employees involved in more strategic decisions.

Getting Started: Stories from High-Involvement Companies

KTA-Tator: Finding Its Footing After Starting Too Big

Sometimes companies start their employee involvement programs with too much ambition. Consider ESOP-owned KTA-Tator, Inc. (KTA) in Pittsburgh, a 300-employee consulting engineering firm that "provides facility owners, architects/engineers, contractors, fabricators, and manufacturers peace of mind that the integrity of steel and concrete structures and other assets are properly assessed and protected."

In late 2018, it attempted to launch a formal Office of Innovation (OI). It encouraged employee-owners with ideas to grow the business to submit their concepts to the OI. The OI was set up like an internal incubator with five phases:

1. 12-week ignition program: A one-hour classroom lesson and homework each week to develop the concept.
2. Investment advisor board: Participants would learn presentation skills necessary to create the business case for their idea and pitch it to an investment panel to determine if the company would underwrite further development.

3. Pilot: Those identified to be viable revenue generating, cost saving, or efficiency improving ideas move onto the pilot program. By this phase ideas would have gone from idea to viable business model. The pilot program would provide a small amount of funding to further develop the idea and bring it to an internal or external test market.
4. Accelerate: Those ideas that show promise in the pilot program would then be refined and moved to the final stage.
5. Full launch: Proven concepts would receive additional resources and be rolled out to a larger targeted market.

The concept was a well-thought out and promising approach—but it proved too big a leap from where the employees were.

CEO Dan Adley told us in February of 2019 that "we got a few ideas from our co-owners, but realized that innovation is something that must be fostered over time. We needed to make innovation less daunting before launching into such an involved program. We also recognized that people think innovation equals disruption. That's too grandiose. Small changes in process that improve efficiency or create a better customer experience are just as important."

So instead, the company will start with a lunch and learn introductory session that will be delivered to staff multiple times over the next quarter. They added an icon on the KTA Bridge (an internal portal that automatically launches when anyone opens their web browser) that prompts co-owners to submit process improvement ideas. Adley said "in introducing it (last month) it was important to explain that this wasn't the traditional 'suggestion box.' We're seeking ideas our co-workers feel will work to improve operations, no matter how large or small. The online submission form helps ensure the concepts are oriented at process improvement."

The new approach is admittedly a modest beginning, and the hope is it can develop further into a farther reaching program.

It will be important for KTA to make sure ideas are responded to quickly with explanations for the action, to let others comment on the ideas, to develop a process where ideas can be moved to ad-hoc teams to address, and to emphasize that identifying problems is just as important or more so than identifying solutions.

Incentives for Ideas at Walman

Walman took a much more traditional approach. Paying employees for ideas is an old idea itself, and one that often does not work very well, generating a limited number of ideas. In a seminal article in the *Harvard Business Review* titled "Why Incentive Plans Cannot Work,"[1] Alfie Kohn argued that paying for performance of any kind results only in temporary change. By creating purely extrinsic motivation, he argues (and cites numerous studies to back up the point) that companies create only temporary compliance, not the more lasting and effective intrinsic motivation that comes from the kind of corporate culture that values ideas and effort and creates a structure where people can find more meaning and purpose in work. A large study in Canada bore Kohn out. Brian Curran and Scott Walsworth concluded that "high performance on complex creative tasks requires intrinsic motivation, and rewards act as a decrement to this motivation."[2]

These studies did not look at ESOP companies, where employees have a long-term interest in how the company does, not just a short-term payoff. Placing the incentives within a corporate culture that values employees may also change the motivational context.

Our experience with companies that have tried this approach is mixed, but what is clear is that these systems can work well if they exist within a clearly elaborated structure that is perceived as fair by employees and is not the only way employees can get involved. That certainly has been true at Walman.

Founded in 1915 and with an ESOP that is over 25 years old, Walman provides diverse products and services to the optical industry, including eye wear, contact lenses, and education. The company is also

1. *Harvard Business Review*, Sept./Oct. 1993.
2. Brian Curran and Scott Walsworth, "Can you pay employees to innovate? Evidence from the Canadian private sector," *Human Resource Management Journal*, July 2014.

a distributor of optical instruments and runs a buying group. Walman's 1,100 employees work in 34 locations, with the greatest number in the Brooklyn Park, Minnesota, manufacturing lab, which runs 24 hours a day.

The New Visions program, which the company has sponsored for over 25 years, pays employees up to 15% of the profit generated by their suggestions in the first year after implementation. Over 770 ideas have been submitted since the program's inception, and one submitted by veteran employee Doug Kryzer resulted in a $40,000 payout.

The New Visions program provides cash incentives based on simple and clearly defined rules. All employees except company officers and people on leaves of absence are eligible to fill out a one-page suggestion form, indicating the issue being addressed, a solution, and a description of the benefit to the company, including the estimated net savings or profit. The program manual says that eligible suggestions contain all four of the following elements:

- Identifies a problem, a potential problem, or an opportunity for the company.
- Presents a solution and potential benefit to the company.
- Identifies where the suggestion has an application.
- The New Visions program form is signed by the suggester(s), includes the suggester's printed name, and is received and dated in the New Visions database.

Sketches, photographs of models, and copies of proposed form changes, statements of financial benefit to the company, etc., if appropriate, must be attached to the form at the time of submission. Items are automatically ineligible when they concern personnel policies, when they are already being considered, when they have already been submitted, or when they include a problem without a solution. Ideas that conflict with company values, company policy, or the company's legal or contractual obligations are also ineligible. (Companies should consider allowing submissions just to identify problems, we think. Just because someone does not have a solution does not mean that identifying a problem is not an essential first step).

The size of the reward depends on whether the suggestion is tangible or intangible. The program manual defines intangible suggestions as ones that "do not result in direct net savings or net profit, cannot be estimated, but improve employee safety, customer relations, customer service, public relations, or working conditions." Tangible rewards are almost uncapped. If a suggestion is adopted, Walman will pay the employee or employees an amount between $50 and $50,000; the actual amount "shall be no more than 15% of the first year's estimated next savings or profit."

If the New Vision committee believes that the size of the savings is uncertain, it may pay the reward in two parts, with the second made after the impact of the suggestion can be observed. Intangible suggestions receive an award based on a point system, up to a maximum of $1,000. In addition, anyone who has submitted an eligible suggestion is entered into a quarterly drawing for $500.

An individual or a group may submit suggestions. If a suggestion is submitted by more than one person, only the first person submitting the suggestion is eligible for a reward. Salaried employees may submit applications, but they will be eligible for a reward only if the suggestion is not related to that employee's responsibilities. Each branch (a branch is a headquarters department or a location outside Minneapolis) has a branch coordinator, who is a non-manager and serves as the liaison for the Employee Ownership Committee and the New Vision committee. The branch coordinator receives a reward equal to 10% of the reward received by the suggester, as long as the coordinator was named on the suggestion form.

An employee fills out the one-page form and hands it in to his or her branch coordinator, who helps the employee improve the idea, if necessary. The suggestion is sent to company headquarters and forwarded anonymously to the New Visions Committee administrator. The idea is then forwarded to the New Visions Committee, which is composed of non-executive employees. It's important to note that the idea is presented to the committee with the employee's name and any specific branch information removed. The committee finds this integral to the decision-making process. The idea is then researched and vetted, which can sometimes take months. If the idea is adopted, the evaluation committee hands it to a task force responsible for implementing the idea within 45 days. Both the employee and his or her branch coordinator receive letters of acknowledgement at each step in the process. Quarterly communications highlight adopted ideas.

The Cargas Systems Shark Tank

Cargas Systems is a software and consulting company based in Lancaster, Pennsylvania, with more than 100 employees who specialize in solutions for accounting and operations, sales and marketing, fuel delivery and service, and custom development. While the company is not owned through an ESOP, more than 70% of the business's employees are shareholders, which has required the personal financial investment of each to a direct stock purchase plan through profit-sharing, bonus distributions, or deductions from pay into a stock purchase savings account for future stock purchases.

Ideas Unlimited is Cargas Systems' friendly, collaborative version of "Shark Tank." This annual event provides a forum for any team member to deliver a presentation to the executive team about any idea—big, small, or off the wall. Creative ideas, creative thinking, and problem-solving have fueled the company's success. The Ideas Unlimited event is its effort to foster an environment that encourages every employee to ask questions, express opinions, make suggestions, and take action to improve the company.

A call for ideas goes out before the event, and those wishing to speak submit a topic and brief description. Presentations are scheduled in 20-minute blocks over two or three days depending on the response. Presenters develop their ideas and create a presentation to deliver. Presentations can be given by individuals or groups, and there is no limit to the number of presentations an employee or group can present.

The executive team, including the president and CEO and business unit vice presidents, attends every presentation, and all other employees are welcome to sit in. Presentations are also recorded so they can be watched after the event. Each presentation includes time for Q&A and discussion so audience members can give feedback. Ideas Unlimited 2017 included presentations about exploring opportunities for the company's fuel delivery software in Canada, applying for B corporation certification, and using virtual reality in their sales process. The event has been the launching pad for numerous initiatives. A presentation about redesigning their website led to the current version of Cargas.com and the creation of CargasEnergy.com for the company's proprietary fuel delivery software. Both sites have changed the way they present their business to the public. A presentation from 2016 to modernize the Cargas Systems logo was carried out in 2017 and launched a larger discussion about their evolving corporate branding. A presentation about cross-selling opportunities led to business unit collaboration initiatives on their 2018 sales plan.

To ensure ideas are acted upon, a follow-up list is sent out after the event. Ideas are divided into categories: those that can be acted on immediately, those that require more development and a dedicated team to lead them, and those that will be part of Cargas' long-term planning and require more in-depth research and input from the executive team. Team members are assigned to take action on each idea and help see it through to fruition. Ideas Unlimited is one of the big initiatives that Cargas has used to strengthen its culture and the ownership mentality, but it certainly isn't the only way Cargas has tried to improve the experience and engagement of its staff. The company values transparency and opens its books, sharing financial and corporate information freely while providing employees with other opportunities to engage in strategic planning and decision making.

The Problem Resolution System at Reflexite

One of the simplest ways to get started is what Reflexite called "EARS (Employee Assistance Response System)." Reflexite was a 550-employee manufacture of reflective products. It grew quickly in its 26 years as an ultimately 100% ESOP, eventually selling at a substantial premium to a

German company in 2011. It was one of the first companies to develop a simple, highly effective employee idea system based on employees submitting an idea or identifying a problem to an employee committee, which took the next steps in deciding how to proceed.

To an outsider, EARS at first appeared to be just a well elaborated suggestion system. The Human Resources manager at the time, Dave Edgar, was adamant that this was not a suggestion system. It was a problem resolution system. Edgar pointed out that suggestion systems put an onus on employees to come up with a solution. More often, however, people just know there is a problem. They may have some ideas on how to solve it, but rarely are they able to work out a detailed and effective plan to deal with it. So many problems never get resolved because the company's official problem solvers (managers, usually) never know there is one.

The EARS system, which is now used and adapted under one name or anther at a number of ESOPs, does look a little like a suggestion system, but in form only. An employee filled out a form that said at the top "The following situation is making it difficult for me to do my job right the first time." The form then got submitted to the EARS coordinator, who was in charge of seeing that it was resolved. All the EARS submissions also went to management in their weekly meetings, along with a status update on the resolution of all the EARS requests.

Unless the problem could be quickly and easily resolved, the EARS coordinator created a "corrective action team (CAT)," an ad hoc committee set up to solve the problem. The team had a coordinator, who may or may not have been an expert in the subject matter but whose charge it was to identify those people who were. People could also volunteer for the teams (all CATs are posted). Teams had a form they filled out reporting on their progress. Almost all participants in CATs were nonmanagement employees.

The teams made decisions about what to do about a problem and presented it to the person who submitted it. An EARS submission could not be put to rest until the submitter agreed the problem had been resolved and signed off on it. Sometimes this process took days; sometimes it took months or longer.

Take the case of Bob Frechette, who came to Reflexite after 16 years in the chemical industry. Frechette, who had a high school education, said that until he came to Reflexite, no one ever cared what he thought at work. At Reflexite, however, he thought the company was wasting too many used chemicals. "What if we got a still," he wondered, "and reused some?" So he put in an EARS, a committee was formed, and Frechette ended up getting a still designed to his specifications. The result? Toxic waste was reduced by 55%, and the company saved $50,000 a year.

An EARS system and those like it has five key elements that make it work so well:

1. It is highly visible, with all submissions being posted.
2. It identifies problems first, then finds solutions.
3. It has a high management priority.
4. It gets employees involved in solutions.
5. It requires that every request be resolved to the requester's satisfaction.

Companies that start with this approach often will add on more elaborated systems for employee involvement, but even if this is the only step a company takes, the results can be dramatic. The next examples look at how companies have created more elaborate, systemic approaches to generating employee ideas.

The Idea Engine at MSA Professional Services

MSA, whose open-book system we visited earlier, also has an ideas process to build on the numbers. In looking to the future, the leadership team of the company asked itself "How will we innovate to create new solutions?" After some discussion and research, they came up with a system intended to harvest ideas from the entire population of the company, and how to go about implementing the best ideas. Rather than seeking large innovative proposals, the company is seeking to leverage the adoption of many small improvements. The new process has been coined the MSA Idea Engine.

A six-person Idea Engine Committee from three locations makes up the ideas team. Team members had previously gone through some Lean training together and were best equipped to implement a process for implementing improvements. The team manages the MSA Idea Engine process of obtaining, reviewing, and steering the implementation of ideas received from within the company. That involves employee huddles, an idea board, ideas email, and a vetting process for the ideas. All employees participate in one or more teams based on their functions.

Huddles by each team in the company are held every month, and at every third huddle (quarterly) there is a goal of generating three ideas per employee. The team then has an idea vetting discussion and then votes for the winner, with each employee getting three votes. The whole process takes 20 to 30 minutes or less. The winning idea from each team is submitted on an idea card that looks like this:

MSA Idea Card

Idea	
Name	Date
What is the problem/waste?	
Why is it happening?	
Idea:	
Date implemented:	

Note that the form asks first to identify the problem. Too often companies only look for solutions, but identifying the problem is the most important step, and vital even if the employees do not have a solution. After all, maybe the team will.

The team leader then maintains an idea board of work in progress:

MSA Idea Board

<table>
<tr><th colspan="5">Idea Board</th></tr>
<tr><td rowspan="2">Huddle day and time</td><td></td><td></td><td></td><td></td></tr>
<tr><td colspan="4">Ideas and Progress</td></tr>
<tr><td rowspan="8">Huddle steps:
1. Review metrics
2. Ideas in progress
3. New ideas
4. Celebrate!</td><td>Idea</td><td>Owner</td><td>Task</td><td>Due Date</td></tr>
<tr><td></td><td></td><td></td><td></td></tr>
<tr><td></td><td></td><td></td><td></td></tr>
<tr><td></td><td></td><td></td><td></td></tr>
<tr><td></td><td></td><td></td><td></td></tr>
<tr><td colspan="4">Follow Up</td></tr>
<tr><td>Parking lot ideas</td><td colspan="2">Needs help that need help [unclear]

Review every three months and move to in progress when a task is assigned.</td><td>Completed ideas</td></tr>
</table>

Parking lot ideas are those that got the second, third, or fourth highest votes, and are revisited at subsequent huddles and discussed for five minutes. Ideas from outside the teams are welcome as well.

The process generates a lot of ideas, but now there needs to be a vetting process to implement them. The Idea Engine Committee can assign subcommittees and designate responsibilities if it believes an idea can be implemented. The idea generator is contacted, and often more information is sought. Subcommittees are synced with the team's schedule.

The evaluation process works on a matrix (see next page). Ideas team leaders send the ideas that are chosen to a designated email, and a tracking systems—the "idea pipeline"—is posted so that everyone can see. The pipeline shows what ideas have been submitted and what their status is.

MSA Idea Vetting Matrix

	Number of Barriers:	
Level of impact:	Low	High
High	Implement Ideas that will be enacted on because they have few barriers and high potential.	Consider Ideas to be investigated further because they have high impact potential but significant barriers.
Low	Possible Ideas that might be acted on because they have few barriers but also limited impact.	Not at this time Ideas that will not be acted on.

MSA CEO Gil Hantzsch said about the process, which only recently launched, "I look forward to seeing the ideas generated by the 'group genius' of our firm implemented. Over the coming years I believe that the aggregation of many small improvements will prove to be more impactful than any one large innovation."

Creating Ideas Processes in Dispersed Workforces

Barclay Water Management, introduced earlier, and NMR, an ESOP-owned energy efficiency assessment company, are two high-involvement companies that have the same problem—most of their workforce is in the field. To get these people involved, both companies developed web-based systems for submitting, commenting on, and tracking ideas. The ideas teams regularly send out updates and encourage participation. At annual all-staff meetings, there are opportunities to review and raise ideas.

The tracking system is meant to generate not just ideas to solve problems, but, probably more important, identifying problems. Too often people are discouraged from raising a problem if they have no solution. The tracking system is set up on a shared platform (there is specific software for this or you can develop your own systems). The idea management platform that incorporates the following features is a kind of interactive spreadsheet. Each company has its own variant of a tracking system, but table 4-2 shows the key elements.

Table 4-2. Key elements in an idea tracking system

Idea or problem	Date submitted	Owner	Likes	Team to address	Reporting by team on progress	Metrics: how well did it work?	Date resolved

In the first column, someone puts in an idea or a problem with a brief explanation. That then goes out to all employees or a selected group. The "owner" is the submitter. Similar to Facebook, in the "likes" column, people who think this is an issue that is important or affects them enters their name and their comments, including if they are willing to be on a team to address it. If there seems to be enough interest (an ideas team should make that decision), then a team is set up of volunteers and often some people who are assigned to it. The group then periodically reports on its progress and resolution, and shares its results with everyone.

Create Your Own Process

By now, you probably expect me to say that these are just examples and you need to craft your own approach. It's true here as it is an all aspects of involvement. There is not a magic formula—there is only what works for you. You will probably start somewhere, realize you need to make changes, and create a new approach.

In doing this, consider the ideas and lessons on how to create employee involvement created by Dallan Guzinski, the NCEO director of ownership culture and engagement. Dallan's annual conference presentation is one of the most popular and impactful sessions of the hundreds held annually. We also look at a simple, quick exercise to generate ideas about getting ideas.

Dallan's Rules for Engagement

The rules for improvisational comedy provide a great template for creating an effective employee ownership culture. Improv is creation and adaptation. We are creating something from nothing every single day in work and in life. So how does improv improve how we do business and culture?

We can use improv for strategy, marketing, and vision. It is great for problem solving and making improvements. It can enhance communications and employee relations. It is the essence of innovation, brainstorming, and teamwork.

Improv works because it addresses the key problem in making teams and culture work. Research by Harvard Business School professor Amy Edmondson found that the two most important traits of effective teams are high involvement and psychological safety—the feeling that people can say what they think in a respectful way and be heard with equal respect. A lack of structure for team-based decision making and fear of looking in some way inappropriate severely undermine Edmonson's two key factors. Improv creates norms and structure where judgment is postponed and participation thrives. It combats fear by creating support, openness, and affirmation.

As an exercise, in a group meeting ask people to think about when they feel the most fear when it comes to failure, making mistakes, expressing themselves openly, or feeling acknowledged or accepted. Similarly, ask people when they have felt the least fear with respect to failure or making mistakes, expressing themselves openly, and feeling acknowledged or accepted.

Then have everyone pair up and imagine they are a couple or friends, and have a conversation about where to go to on vacation. Person one's suggestion ("Let's go hiking in Alberta") has to be met with a "Yes, but..." response ("Yes, but we always go hiking"), which person one will respond to with another but ("Yes, but we love hiking," followed by another "Yes, but..." ("I'd rather do something more cultural this year"), etc., etc. Do this for one or two quick, and likely frustrating, minutes. Now try the same conversation with a new rule: the response must be "yes, and...." "Let's go hiking in Yosemite" is followed by a "yes, and..." ("Yes, and I'd love to do one with waterfalls"), which is perhaps followed by ("Yes, and maybe we can take a side trip to the redwoods). Key to this exercise is that people should support and respect what their partner has created. When done, ask people how they felt about the two conversations.

The Rules of Improv follow a few basic principles:

1. Agree, Don't Deny.
2. "YES, AND..."
3. Make Statements (Or... Support Your Teammates)
4. There Are No Mistakes

Rule 1: Agree, Don't Deny: This creates a space of safety to share ideas or provide input. Postpone judgement and respect what your partner has created. Ask people to pair off and decide where to go out to dinner [your examples are about vacations]. First, make sure that all the statements are based on agreement (it's fair to do what you want this year). Then switch to denying (I hate the hot weather). Ask how people feel they feel this way (maybe a bit uneasy).

Rule 2: Yes, And: Now do the same thing but each statement is "yes, and." So maybe say that's a good idea, and maybe we can take a side trip. And the second person says yes, and we can try to go camping there. Each person tries to find a way to make the "and" work for both sides.

Rule 3: Make statements: Support your teammates... don't exhaust them. Take the pressure off team members by contributing more (and they will do the same for you). Include yourself; focus on solutions, not your team's obstacles. Don't be too quick to edit. Risk aversion and negativity will inhibit innovation and willingness to participate in the creative process.

Rule 4: There are no mistakes. Mistakes are inevitable, so rather than view them as failure, look for the learning opportunity. Stop playing the blame game. Jack Stack of the Great Game of Business adds his own rules here:

- Myth 1: Nice guys finish last.
- Myth 2: A manager's job is to come up with all the answers.

"Build confidence in other people," Stack says. "To do that, you have to show people you're human, you're not God, you don't have all the answers, you make a lot of mistakes."

As an exercise to see how this works, have people think back on a time when they or their team experienced failure. Try to extract three different positive outcomes from that experience.

Exercises like this may seem awkward at first, bit with practice, they can help build the kind of trust and safety essential for ownership culture.

Dallan's exercise helps lay the groundwork for how to participate. Now consider step two: the ideas process exercise. The goal here is to bring people together to help to find a process to create your own ideas team approach. You may recall we visited this idea before as a way to find out how employees might participate more. Now the idea is to use it to address specific ideas for any work issue (quality, process control, marketing, etc.). So you won't have to look back, it is repeated here.

Start by dividing everyone at the meeting (this may be the whole workforce or some part of it) into randomly assigned tables of eight or so people (you can have them count off). The steps for the exercise follow:

1. Designate a reporter.
2. Have each person take 60 seconds to write down one or more ideas on what makes it difficult for an employee with an idea or a problem that is not being resolved to move it forward.
3. Have each person very briefly state what he or she wrote down.

4. Have the group choose the two most important ideas mentioned.
5. Now repeat the process but ask each individual to write down what could be done to make it easier to share the idea or problem. It is critical here that the answer not be a vague concept like "management should listen," or "we need to communicate better." The focus has to be on a specific thing that can be implemented, such as having a daily huddle or weekly team meeting.
6. Have the group pick the top two ideas.
7. Go around the room and ask each reporter to identify one barrier, then repeat for the second one (you will find a lot of the same issues get raised in round two).
8. Do the same for solutions.

This process will yield at least a few good suggestions, but it is only the starting point. Your ideas team can use these ideas as anchors for this process, adding its own take on what to do next. The process can be repeated periodically as the company gains experience. The goal is to make sure that employees feel some ownership of the new processes that emerge.

Whatever approach you start with, understand that as people gain experience, the processes that work will need to change as well. The goal to keep in mind is always the same—find ways to generate more good ideas from more people about more things.

Phelps County Bank, a 100% long-time ESOP in Rolla, Missouri, took this journey. It started its employee involvement process with something very much like EARS. The program was in place for many years, and helped Phelps become a strikingly successful company. Phelps sent all its employees to the kind of training that only managers usually get. It shared the numbers on all sorts of metrics. Employee ideas ranged from creating a play area for kids so parents could spend more time with customer service agents to learn about Phelps services to ideas for new products the bank might offer.

Over time, the process faded away, not because it was not working, but because the concept of forming an ad hoc team to investigate an idea became so second nature than employees just did it without needing an intermediary process. That informal approach worked for them; it might not work for you. Constantly assessing how you are doing is the only way to know.

KEY TAKEAWAYS

1. Getting ideas requires more than just allowing them. It requires a specific structure.
2. In creating a structure for idea generation, you will get more employee buy-in if you have an ideas team or other group of employees participate in the process.
3. Ambiguity as to what employees can decide, where they can have only input, and where they have no role other than to be informed can create cynicism and withdrawal. Map these decisions out carefully and explain why you are doing it that way.
4. Start with what will work for you and build on success. Starting with a very ambitious plan too quickly carries a greater risk of failure.
5. Incentives for ideas will work for some companies and not for others, but they always need a specific structure that leads employees to develop ideas.
6. Ideas that go beyond simple, "no-brainer" changes should be charted with indicators for who is responsible, progress, goals, metrics, and status.
7. You can have employee involvement even in dispersed workforces. Web-based tracking systems and meeting apps can make this easier.
8. Use exercises like the ones in this chapter to give employees a context for how to share ideas and get feedback on the best way to do it.

CHAPTER 5

Work-Level Teams

No matter how you slice it, almost inevitably, employee involvement revolves around work-level teams. They may be permanent teams in common work areas, ad hoc teams that are created to address a specific issue then dissolve when it is resolved, or cross-functional teams on issues like product development or safety.

In developing a team-based system, you need to identify which issues can best be resolved by employees meeting on a regular basis. Not all issues benefit from group discussions. For those that do, you need to be unambiguous about what their authority is, how they are structured, who leads them, and who they report to. Some teams may be created specifically to find new solutions or develop new products or processes; others may be more focused on improving existing systems, monitoring performance against metrics, and making sure any anticipated problems are addressed. Often, team meetings are check-ins just to talk about what has worked and what needs working on.

To get started, management or (if there is one) an employee ownership steering committee or ideas team should select what work areas of the company need more employee involvement and set up work groups by area.

There are a lot of potential approaches to how to decide where and how teams function. It may just be that management and the ideas team make these decisions. But this may be more effective if you start by finding out what employees think.

For instance, you can have a company-wide meeting or just a meeting of selected people from around the company attend a session that will probably last 90 minutes or more. If a large number of employees is involved, a representative group probably needs to be designated (perhaps by selective volunteering, where people can voluntarily join the process, but some people who need to be involved are specifically asked to join). Ideally, each work area would be represented by about six to twelve employees. If you have multiple locations, this process would be replicated at each one.

Each team of employees would be asked to designate a group leader and recorder. The employees should then be given a handout asking them to discuss the issue of how to increase effective employee input into decisions affecting their work area. They should be asked to decide (and record their decisions) on the following issues:

- Who should be involved?
- What is the scope of their authority (can they just make recommendations or can they actually make decisions on some or all issues)?
- What specific issues can the group take up?
- How can problems be identified for the group to consider? Can or should employees submit them on a form to the group? Should management be able to ask the group to address certain issues?
- Is a budget needed? How much and what for?
- Should people from outside their work area be involved in some or all meetings? If yes, who?
- How will the meetings be run? Where? When? How often? Who will facilitate them?
- Who will take the lead in organizing details of the process?
- How will meetings, and their results, be communicated to employees?
- Should involvement be voluntary or mandatory?
- Should meetings be on an ad hoc or regularly scheduled basis?
- Who will measure effectiveness, and how will that be done?
- What information will the group need to make good decisions?
- How can the process be changed as people learn what works and what doesn't?

Have each group report back a synopsis of its discussion. Now reexamine the issue with the entire group of participants to see what seems like would work. This discussion can then guide the ideas team and management in deciding where to start or, if you already have teams, how to improve them. Periodic reevaluation is essential. As I have noted, as people get better at employee involvement, the structures that will work will often need to be changed and improved. And if they don't get better, obviously changes are urgently needed.

An alternative or supplement to this effort can be to send out a survey to employees asking then to respond to these issues. As with all surveys, it is critical that you report back what people said and what you will do as a result.

Common Problems in Teams

Despite all their advantages, however, teams do not automatically make better decisions. There are a few key problems to be particularly vigilant about:

- *Groupthink:* We have all been involved in a process in which a group forms a consensus around the views of its most vocal members—even if their arguments are not well supported. Contrary arguments are not considered seriously, or even sought. Dissidents are seen as disruptive or disloyal. Information contrary to the group view is discounted or ignored. The group may even develop a sense of moral certainty and superiority. Groupthink often emerges where there are very strong leaders and an unequal distribution of power.
- *Excess faith in consensus:* Groups of all stripes tend to work through consensus. That has many advantages, but it can also mean that the maverick ideas that turn out to be real breakthroughs can be discouraged. It also can push decisions to the least common denominator, not the optimal solution. There is a powerful logic behind accepting a solution we can all live with, even if it is not the best one.

- *Negative geniuses:* Research shows that the most negative people in a group are usually seen as the smartest, creating a bias to inaction. After all, it's a lot easier to raise reasons something might not work than to suggest taking a chance on a risky high-return idea.
- *The wrong issues:* Groups can spend too much time on things they either don't know much about (those who are expert should just decide), that aren't important enough to merit their time, that they don't have any authority to deal with anyway, or that are not improved by having discussions.
- *Lack of follow-through:* All too often, promising ideas get generated but there is no specific plan of action to implement them. That may be because management has that responsibility and either has other priorities or just disagrees and does not want to say so. If it is the team's responsibility, there may be no process for assigning tasks and following up on them. Finally, even with the best plans for action, nothing can happen without adequate resources and a plan of follow-up that assigned specific tasks to specific people. As Will Rogers once said, "a vision without a plan is a hallucination."
- *Poor team leadership:* Leading a team takes skills and often training. The goal cannot be for the leader to make or even guide the decisions; the goal is for the leader to make it possible for other people to reach them.

Problems with teams have been dissected at length in many useful books, such as *The New Why Teams Don't Work* by Harvey Robbins and Michael Finley and Patrick Lencioni's *The Five Dysfunctions of Teams*. The authors all are strong team advocates but explain how it can easily fail and how to avoid it.

To make the teams work better, it helps to be aware of the key problems and take steps to avoid them, including:

- Have a designated advocate for ideas and maybe a designated critic.
- Train group leaders (it may just be mentoring from other leaders who are good at it).

- Make sure the team knows what ideas it can implement and which ones need approval, and that the team has the resources to implement the ideas it is allowed to implement on its own.
- Encourage people in positions of authority to be deferential to other ideas or perhaps not even join some group meetings.
- Make sure dissenters don't get punished just for disagreeing.
- Set rules for when the group can make decisions other than by consensus.

It's also important to think through where certain groups make sense and where they don't. Which decisions require that only people with specific technical expertise be involved—even if it is just one person? Which decisions are too prone to the dynamics mentioned above to let the group have the final say? Having a team periodically evaluate group decisions to see where the process seemed excessively conservative, slow, trivial, or negative may help identify issues that should be moved elsewhere.

Despite all this, the vast majority of businesses err far too much on the other side, involving employees in too few significant work-level decisions. In fact, the fear of these problems has kept too many organizations solidly mired in the bureaucratic command-and-control model, a decision process whose problems are all too well known.

Sometimes companies embark on employee involvement programs only to run into a stone wall from managers, supervisors, and/or employees. "We tried that before," they say, "and it just didn't work." A lot of this frustration has to do with the inevitable ambiguity that arises when people's roles change. Managers and supervisors now are supposed to coach and listen; employees to share ideas and information.

Defining these new roles can be difficult, but it is essential to developing realistic expectations of just what participation involves. Typically, there's a learning curve for each of the groups. Management needs to learn how to balance giving up control while continuing to provide leadership. Middle managers must learn to give up some authority and become catalysts for employee input and decision making. Employees need to learn new skills that will allow them to contribute. Lastly, each group needs to understand how everyone else contributes.

One way to address these issues is to get people together in small groups, with representation from each group at each table. You will need a facilitator to lead the exercise. Have each group think of an example in the company where employee participation was tried. Now ask each member to take on the role of someone representing a point of view different than their own. For example, a nonmanagement employee will act as a senior manager or supervisor, a middle manager will become a nonmanagement employee or senior manager, and the senior manager will act as a nonmanagement employee or supervisor.

Have each group discuss the participation effort from the point of view they represent based on the following:

- Who had input into the design and implementation?
- How was the effort communicated?
- Did you have enough information? Was it understandable?
- Did you understand what your role was?
- Did you get involved?
- Did you support the effort?
- Did you have training to help you adjust to the change?
- Were you able to discuss your concerns with management, supervisors, and employees?
- Were comments thoughtful or just venting frustration?
- Was enough time given?
- Was there a system for feedback and follow-through?
- Were the goals clear and achievable?
- Were the necessary resources available?
- Did you feel appreciated? Is that a reasonable expectation?

Have each group report back a synopsis of its discussion. Now reexamine the issue with the entire group of participants to see what was effective and where improvements could have been made. Whether the participation effort was successful or not, there's something to be learned from analyzing it in this way.

Psychological Safety

A massive research project at Google looked at what factors determine whether teams work. The most important factor turned out to be a sense of psychological safety, the belief among team members that they can express their views without being disrespected. This does not mean other factors, such as skilled facilitators, clear authority, and diversity in view and traits of team members, do not matter as well, but psychological safety matters most.

In her book *The Fearless Organization*,[1] mentioned in chapter 2, Amy Edmondson provides a succinct way to accomplish this; see table 5-1, previously seen as table 2-1 in chapter 2.

Table 5-1. The leader's toolkit for psychological safety

	Setting the stage	Inviting participation	Responding productively
Leadership tasks	**Frame the work** • Set expectations about failure, uncertainty, and interdependence to clarify the need for voice **Emphasize purpose** • Identify what's at stake, why it matters, and for whom it matters	**Demonstrate situational humility** • Acknowledge gaps **Practice inquiry** • Ask good questions • Model intense listening **Set up structures and processes** • Create forums for input • Provide guidelines for discussion	**Express appreciation** • Listen • Acknowledge and thank **Destigmatize failure** • Look forward • Offer help • Discuss, consider, and brainstorm next steps **Sanction clear violations**
Accomplishes	Shared expectations and meaning	Confidence that voice is welcome	Orientation toward continuous learning

1. Amy Edmondson, *The Fearless Organization* (Hoboken, NJ: Wiley, 2019).

Another useful approach is to follow the rules of improv. Dallan Guzinski of the NCEO, whom we met earlier, describes how these rules can help teams function better.

Improvisational comedy relies on a set of rules meant to create both continuity and surprise. Presented with a scenario, improv players usually rely in part on things they have done together before, just as employees do in a company.

Employees trying to come up with new ideas or solve old problems face a similar scenario. In a traditional firm, they just rely on the old routines, changing only when told by management. But in a high-involvement situation, they need to improvise something new. Sometimes that will mean veering off in a whole new direction; often it is making changes at the edges of what is being done now—our old friend the adjacent possible. Using improv rules provides some useful guidelines. Improv helps create safe spaces for participation by combating fear and creating support, openness, and affirmation.

Because fear is the biggest impediment to participation, creative thinking, and healthy relationships at work, setting norms for how to minimize it is a necessary prerequisite for success. The Improv exercise is one way to model these norms.

Start by asking employees to think about (and maybe write down and share) when they have felt the most fear when it comes to:

- Expressing yourself openly and honestly
- Making mistakes
- Being bold or taking risks
- Using imagination
- Feeling validated or accepted

Do the exercise we discussed above in Dallan's rules to get people attuned to "yes, and" thinking. Saying "yes and" like this is of greatest value in brainstorming. Obviously, it is not normally a way to make a final decision because it involves too little critical judgment and too many compromises. But as a way to get ideas out there, it works very well. It creates a space where people feel safe to share ideas or provide input while judgment is postponed. People should be reminded to practice "yes and" as the default response when hearing any idea from anyone, rather than immediately thinking of why something cannot be done. On the flip side, now that you are making the effort to create this safe space, people need to know it is their job to contribute ideas.

In using this approach for brainstorming, keep a few rules in mind:

- Make concise statements: Support your teammates... don't exhaust them. Statements encourage confidence and participation.
- Remember that identifying problems is as or more important than identifying solutions.
- Focus on the positive first. Don't be too quick to edit. People are risk averse, and negativity will inhibit innovation and willingness to participate in the creative process.
- There are no mistakes, only ideas.
- One of the most important lessons from the Google research is that effective teams make systematic efforts to ensure all people have a chance to talk. That may need to be structured into the meeting.

Anne Claire Broughton, an organizational development consultant who now also heads the North Carolina Employee Ownership Center, told our 2018 annual conference that creating safety does not mean avoiding conflict at all costs. Doing that can lead to excessively conservative, second-best approaches and an inability to adapt to change.

She told the audience that "one of the most important things a company must do to create an effective high involvement culture is to learn to deal with conflict productively. This enables different perspectives to be voiced, leading to more rigorous thought and better decisions (and avoiding group-think). People get to be heard even if their ideas don't carry the day, so they are more likely to support the prevailing decision. Relationships are reinforced and innovation is encouraged."

Broughton imagines creating a decision-making map where people's different perspectives are heard until they create what author Sam Kaner calls a "groan zone" where ideas start to conflict. Broughton says that "a productive process will start to narrow these perspectives to create a new common understanding. The key is to understand that the discomfort of the groan zone is what lets you think in new ways."

Once the brainstorming is over, of course, you need to bring some critical judgment. To continue to make people feel safe, focus on the best ideas, making it clear that that does not mean other ideas do not have some merit. Colleagues and managers can also use this approach in day-to-day interactions, always looking as much as possible to build on some nugget of usefulness in an idea rather than just saying "that won't work," or "we tried that before."

These abstract principles and exercises may provide guidance to help make your teams more effective, but, as throughout this book, the easiest way to see how teams put ideas into action is to look at what ESOP companies are doing. Some of these ideas may work for you or at least give you a good start.

Company Examples

Kaizen at Flinchbaugh Engineering

Kaizen is a continuous improvement process first developed in Japan but now used worldwide. One of its distinguishing features is that it involves all employees, which makes it a good fit for employee ownership companies. Kaizen has six core concepts:

- Standardize an operation.
- Measure the standardized operation (cycle times or quality standards in manufacturing; customer service processes for a retailer, etc.).
- Gauge measurements against requirements for profits, productivity, or whatever other critical number is being used.
- Get employees involved in finding innovative ways to improve performance.
- Standardize the new, improved operations.
- Continue the cycle repeatedly.

A kaizen blitz is an intensive process over a few to several days to address a problem or seek a new opportunity.

In most companies, management defines the standards and employee teams then work to improve on them, often through small changes made continuously. In employee ownership companies, however, employee teams may themselves set the standards. A major part of the process is the mapping of the work process, often visually. Employees are usually asked first to brainstorm lots of ideas before the teams start to discuss them to agree on a new approach. Flinchbaugh Engineering (FEI), a 100% ESOP contract manufacturing company in York, Pennsylvania, has put an employee ownership spin on the process.

Mike Deppen, FEI's controller, says the kaizen committee meets every two weeks to review suggestions, welcoming ideas for major process improvements and simpler "ah-ha" suggestions, such as moving the company's mailbox. The committee implements the ideas and publishes them. FEI also works on frequent "kaizen blitz" projects. In 2018, the company had 482 kaizen suggestions submitted by 93% of its work force. Flinchbaugh has an annual profit-sharing program, and the number of individual continuous improvement proposals submitted is a factor in the calculation of the shareholder's annual profit-sharing amount. The total company kaizen proposals submitted for the full year of 2018 totaled an impressive $1.5 million—or, given how stock value is a multiple of earnings, several million more in stock price.

Hypertherm

Hypertherm (discussed above) is a New Hampshire-based ESOP company that manufactures industrial cutting systems and software used in industries such as shipbuilding, construction, and automotive repair to cut metal, stone, and similar material. In total, the company employs more than 1,400 people—"associates" in Hypertherm-speak—throughout the world. Its culture and triple-bottom line approach to business is widely lauded with the company earning numerous workplace awards. Accolades include recognition as one of *Forbes* magazine's Best Midsize Employers in 2018, and Employee Owned Company of the Year by the

New England ESOP Association in 2019. Its ESOP owns 100% of the company.

Hypertherm is highly focused on creating a participative culture and providing the training needed to make it work. The organization uses a matrix structure with three groups of teams. Functional teams, such as finance and human resources, support the entire organization; business teams focus on a particular family of products, contributing extensive product expertise; and regional teams, divided by global region, are charged with a deep understanding of the company's customers. If one team has excess capacity, it can send associates to other teams in need of resources.

Within these broad teams, smaller teams of employees at all levels meet regularly to submit ideas, called "continuous improvement activities," or CIAs, for making the company better. As we noted at the outset of this book, each year more than 2,000 ideas are submitted, of which about three-quarters are implemented. Teams themselves are charged with the responsibility of bringing their own ideas into practical use. They are empowered to make decisions that will bring not only short-term, but long-term business results.

Leaders for the teams are generally internally developed and identified by the management team. Associates receive extensive training to help them take a more active role, part of which is traditional skills training to allow employees to perform multiple jobs. Associates spend an average of about 17 hours per year in training. Orientation for new associates is extensive, and every associate receives team training skills as well. Leadership training is designed around competencies and is required of all leaders. In addition to the initial leadership training of 50 hours, there are continuous leadership development opportunities available.

The company also practices open-book management, posting month-end EBIT results on bulletin boards and holding company-wide quarterly meetings for financial updates. As part of the strategic planning process, the teams identify their "KBIs" (key business indicators) and their measures for performance, ensuring buy-in among all team members.

SRC Mini-Games

The SRC Mini-Game model has been widely copied by ESOP companies. Mini-Games are short-term, intensely focused improvement campaigns designed to effect a change, correct a weakness, or pursue an opportunity within the company. The teams that "play" a mini-game can vary in size based on the goal, but usually are small. Over time, almost everyone at SRC will be involved in multiple mini-games. Each has a goal, a scoreboard, and a reward for winning. Rewards are typically something fun, not a major financial incentive.

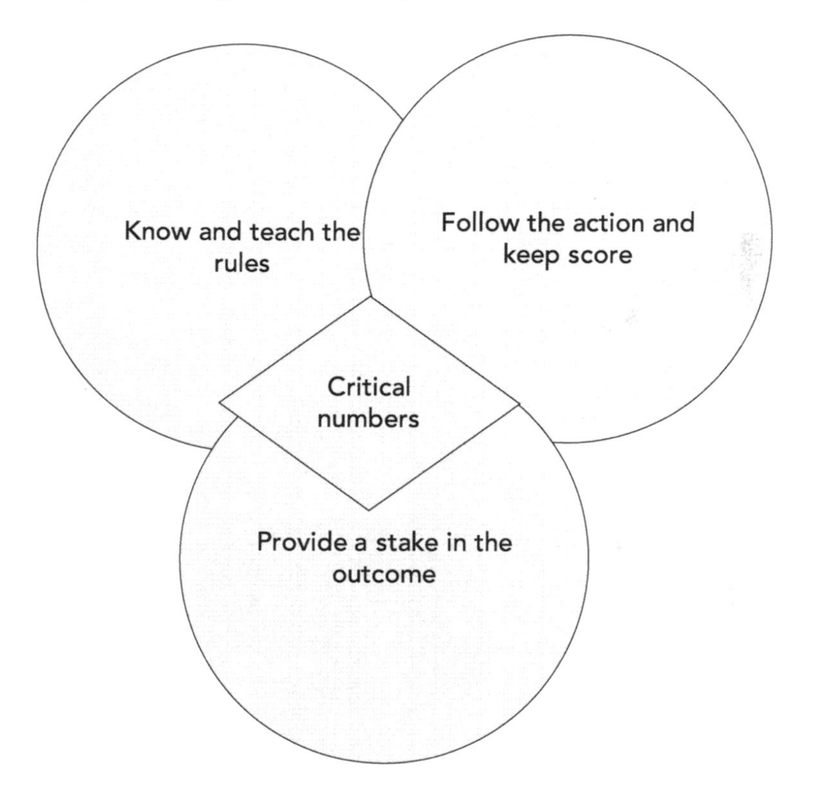

Figure 5-1. The rules of the Game

- Step One: Name the Game: Choose key targets and identify goals. Think "line of sight" and don't compete with "us," the overall goals of the organization.

- Step Two: Define where the least effort gets the biggest impact. Define the win and set how it will be measured. Avoid all-or-nothing objectives.
- Step Four: Estimate the benefit.
- Step 4: Identify the players and form a team of employees involved in the particular issue. In many cases, there will already be a team of employees at your company, such as a production or quality control team.
- Step 5: Set the time frame.
- Step 6: Create a theme and build the scoreboard.
- Step 7: Decide the reward.
- Step 7: Establish the rhythm (how often do you meet for how long and what goes into each meeting).
- Step 9: Play the game.
- Step 10: Celebrate the win.

Mini-games often last a few weeks to a few months. Once an issue is resolved, there is usually a new process that can be used long-term and may be useful for other teams as well. The teams dissolve when done so that people are not meeting just to meet.

Radian Research

Radian Research in Lafayette, Indiana, is a 100% ESOP-owned manufacturer of metrology products, primarily for the utility industry. Radian meters are used to make sure that the power meters utilities and others use to measure energy usage are accurately performing those measures.

Radian CEO Tim Everidge was impressed with what he saw at other ESOP companies and how they were using self-managing teams to drive performance. After some experimentation, Radian settled on five teams designated by the product families of shop products, site products, lab products, software products, and customer service. The teams were staffed based on a mix of different departments, a mix of personalities and experience, and a sprinkle of product expertise. Using these criteria, selections were made from the various employees who volunteered and a few who were "voluntold."

The system has been in place for over a year and is starting to deliver important results, but it has been a learning process to get them working right.

Everidge says the issues that have presented difficulties include:

- Gathering relevant data
- Pulling in other resources when needed
- Fearing they might be stepping on toes of others
- Delegating work to each other
- Learning how to be empowered

Teams meet biweekly and record and report progress in monthly scoreboard meetings. The teams provide quarterly reports to the executive team.

In a short time, Everidge says, the teams have resolved several production issues, saving tens of thousands of dollars. For instance, knowing customer issues and who the customer is has improved the involvement and mindset of employees. That mindset goes back to their work areas. Assembly processes are being changed due to this involvement, and it is driven by the employees.

Because the teams are cross-functional, communication between departments has improved, resulting in a better team effort. Everidge says a number of areas have improved:

- Much better communication between departments.
- Greater awareness of product / service issues and exactly who is affected.
- More proactive approach to improving on quality, delivery, and cost.
- Greater feeling of involvement and knowledge of the impact of that work.

- People feel they are getting involved with issues and are part of the solution.
- Employees who do not normally see or hear about customer issues are now exposed to that information and are directly involved in finding solutions.
- Employees are showing more interest and focus on customer issues.
- There is team involvement. As the SMTs (self-managed teams) have evolved over the last year, the team members have been involved in improving the process. Each team member "owns" issues and reports on them during team meetings.

Everidge sees this as just the start. One key goal is to use the self-managing teams to improve not just existing processes, but to identify and develop new business opportunities. The team-based approach means that customers now deal not just with sales but with a group of people from all areas of the company, making it easier to zero in on the intersection of what is needed and what is possible.

One key lesson from Radian is that having people from different areas on the teams makes them more creative as well as more effective in making sure that any new ideas will work across boundaries. Of course, some teams (including at Radian) are more traditionally focused just around one work area, such as a particular product line.

Conclusion

Teams are the essence of employee involvement. Having people get together in a regular, structured way to identify problems, track progress, and make decisions or at least provide ideas makes getting more good ideas from more people about more things much more likely. But getting teams to work well can be tricky. People may feel the team meetings are taking them away from "real work." Some managers will feel threatened. Team dynamics may lead to second-best decisions, groupthink, domination by a few people, and other dysfunctions. It takes persistence to find what works for you. But not using teams at all is guaranteed not to work.

KEY TAKEAWAYS

- Don't start too large—start where you can be confident of early success so people will see results.
- Create a sense of psychological safety in teams. If people are afraid or insecure about expressing ideas, a few people will dominate.
- Be aware of typical team dysfunctions, such as groupthink, negativity bias, lack of follow through, and having too much faith in experts.
- Try starting with interactive exercises to have employees help identify possible team structures.
- Consider using improv exercises to set the stage for effective brainstorming.
- Learn what other companies are doing by visiting nearby companies and/or going to conference sessions.
- Mini-games are an easy, effective way to address specific issues through a team process.
- Consider the value of having diverse areas and people on your teams.
- Be ready to evaluate and change how your teams work.

CHAPTER 6

Beyond Work Teams: Getting Employees Involved in Strategic Planning

The ultimate step in employee involvement is involving employees in strategic planning. Strategic plans are almost always developed by a select group of managers who then ask employees to implement them. But an employee ownership company that has made the effort to teach employees how to understand and use the numbers and that is generating a lot of ideas on day-to-day work-level issues has a significant resource it can use at the strategic level as well.

At the very least, employees will be able to provide input and feedback on how new initiatives might be received by employees, suppliers, and customers. Will there be resistance, or will they be embraced? What kinds of practical nuts-and-bolts problems might arise in implementation? Beyond that, employees may have ideas on new initiatives themselves. Often, these may come from their interactions with customers or suppliers or perhaps ideas they have seen from other places they have worked. Even if a lot of these ideas are rejected, just a few good ones can make a huge difference in how a company performs.

On the other side, new initiatives are only as effective as the people carrying them out. If employees are not receptive to them, even good ideas may falter. But if they feel like they have had a seat at the table, they are much more likely to buy in.

The kind of strategic planning described here is not the very high-level plan developed by top management for issues such as major new market initiatives, capital budgets, acquisitions, staffing, etc. Instead, it harkens back to Steven Johnson's idea of the adjacent possible. It seeks to involve employees in identifying and responding to practical opportunities, evaluated in a matrix that looks like this:

Issue	How identified
Market niches and opportunities for new products	Conversations with customers and potential customers; trade show research
Process and quality improvements	Conversations with fellow workers
Marketing opportunities for existing products	Conversations with customers and potential customers; trade show research
Changes in organization of work	Conversations with fellow workers

Once opportunities have been identified, evaluation is based on determining:

- Do we have the necessary resources (employee skills, capital, technology, etc.)?
- If not, can we develop them?
- What would be the payback from deploying these resources?
- Even if the idea can pay for itself, is there a higher use for these resources that would be better?

This process would ideally involve a multi-functional approach with people from different areas of the company (such as marketing, production, and engineering in a manufacturing company) meeting to explore opportunities and make decisions.

In this chapter, we look at how a few diverse veteran ESOP companies have involved employees at the strategic level.

KTA-Tator: A Flexible Approach to High-Involvement Planning

We started the chapter on ideas teams with KTA-Tator's first step in creating a process. The company is also a good starting point for high-involvement planning. Their process has a specific structure, but it is flexible and intuitive. Let Dan Adley (KTA-Tator's CEO) explain:

> Our annual strategic planning process produces 3–5 key strategic initiatives that must be pursued in the following year to move us toward our overarching 5-year goals. The champion and team members for each key strategy (KS) come from participants in the strategic planning session (managers and senior professionals from each business unit). However, each KS team is tasked to reach into the organization to identify and recruit "influencers" from among all stakeholders. We are in the process of creating a hybrid organizational structure where organically formed "networks" coexist with a more traditional hierarchical organization. In networks, individuals with the largest numbers of informal, personal connections to other members of their clustered team are usually the most powerful. These are the people we refer to as "influencers." Influencers have power because of social contagion. That is, the number of other people who are regularly exposed to their viewpoints and feel a valued personal connection to the influencer is high. Determining who these influencers are can be counterintuitive, because the org chart's leader is often not the influencer in his or her cluster/silo. Rather, it's likely a subordinate who has been a part of the organization for many years and has garnered the respect of peers and associates.
>
> So each KS team is tasked to identify "influencers" and gain their insights as the KS team addresses their initiative. The thought is that if you want to be successful in the end, it is essential that any narrative coming out of KS teams be targeted at and communicated with these influencers. Without getting and maintaining traction with influencers, the changes KS teams envision will stall. Identifying influencers that can carry the message to the organization increases the likelihood of adoption. This is the first year of focus on a network component of our organization. Influencers are getting to hear about the work of the KS teams, perhaps even influence their direction, and with their buy-in they help disseminate the message, organically. It's too early to tell how well this will work, but initial results are promising.

The Radian Research Ideas to Innovation ("I2I") Process

As we saw in the last chapter, Radian has been moving quickly to a high-involvement management process, but in 2019, as this book was being written, it wanted to go further and get more people involved in strategy development. We asked Tim Everidge, Radian's CEO, to describe it. He responded in detail, as follows:

> In 2018, an all-employee led SWOT (strengths, weaknesses, opportunities, and threats) analysis identified a concern for the lack of innovation. Agreeing that this was an issue, leadership did a thorough analysis, leading to a change in our business model. The sales team unofficially transitioned from a focus on selling existing products only to spending more time listening to customers, being observant and curious about changing customer needs, and communicating those needs back to the appropriate individuals at the company. Until this change, we had lost touch with the customer and did not know what new products should be developed to meet changing customer needs. Moreover, unofficial gate keepers became empowered and made decisions on what new products would be developed with minimal to no customer input. That meant competitors now were disrupting our market, and while we were still doing reasonably well, we would need to change to grow.
>
> The result was a new model with six steps:
>
> 1. Identify the problem and understand the underlying details.
> 2. Redefine the business model with the mindset that innovation starts at the point of contact with the customer.
> 3. Create an official process structure for successful execution of the business model.
> 4. Communicate to the internal staff what the official business model is and the process structure.
> 5. Live the business model and follow the process structure.
> 6. Evaluate the progress and determine what corrections need to be implemented.

We went live with the "Ideas to Innovation" ("I2I") initiative in April 2019.

The New Process

New opportunity ideas typically come from the field sales staff and are channeled through the Ideas to Innovation (I2I) review team consisting of the VP of sales and marketing, the manager of engineering, the VP of finance, and the CEO, with the CEO having final decision making authority. The I2I Review Team meets every week to review the status of the current list of opportunities and to evaluate new opportunities for classification such as: do not pursue, needs more market research, needs more engineering feedback, or approved as an active project. If it is approved as an active project, then the chief engineer (typically) leads the technical effort on execution of the project. If it is outside of the scope of knowledge of the chief engineer, then the appropriate talent is brought in. To be granted approved status, the proposed idea must be a fit within the company's existing product portfolio or it must be strategically tangential allowing for a logical market/product expansion, and it must assist in increasing revenues either directly or indirectly.

The desire is to listen to customers to create a more agile product development that can quickly respond to customer requests with applied engineering by using existing technology blocks already used in other company products. That allows a new product solution to be released in less than six months with most being less than three months. Ideas requiring research and development are generally in the time range of one to three years for the new product to be released.

The chief engineer has the primary responsibility once the I2I review team approves an idea. The chief engineer reports to the VP of sales and marketing and is not (generally) involved with any long-term research and development projects. Instead the focus is on quick turn customer solutions, and his full title is "chief engineer, special projects" to emphasize the desired focus. In most situations the chief engineer with a technician can complete the quick turn project. There are times, though, when additional technical resources may be needed. In those cases, the chief engineer requests the specialized resources from the engineering manager. Many times engineers who are assigned to larger research and development projects have intermittent availability as they wait for another engineer(s) to finish a portion of the project. The idea is to apply this intermittent availability to short-term projects for a quick turn solution that helps keep Radian close to its customers while growing annual revenues.

I2I in Action

The following are examples of how "Ideas to Innovation" operates:

A customer requested a new testing solution from Radian. The I2I review team determined it needed more information from the customer, causing a follow-up discussion including the chief engineer to understand more details about the desired solution. The I2I review team and chief engineer determined that the desired product had no new technology and could be completed using applied engineering. Radian provided drawings to the customer to illustrate the proposed solution. Customer B came back with some desired modifications to the packaging. Radian responded with the modifications to the illustrations. The customer came back and stated that they wanted to order both versions. The I2I evaluation team determined that both versions could be viable products that other customers would be interested in. Radian is now awaiting the purchase order.

Another customer was experiencing challenges with throughput in their operation and did not have enough employees to do all the work. Details of this came out during a discussion with the Radian regional sales manager. The I2I review team determined that this was an opportunity to provide a service that would later likely result in product sales. The vice president of sales and marketing has a black belt certification in "Transactional Process Improvement," and the I2I review team believed that this knowledge could be leveraged into a new service offering by the company. Moreover, we think other customers are experiencing the same challenges. A quotation/proposal was provided for the service of a three-day process improvement workshop, resulting in a purchase order for the service. The training resulted in the customer wanting to discuss Radian products in general. After completion of the project, we started marketing this more widely. We have already received the second purchase order from another customer, and the subsequent process improvement workshop has been scheduled.

Next Steps for Radian Research

The process Tim Everidge describes above yielded multiple new opportunities in just the first few months. The next step will be to broaden the process to create a company-wide approach where employees at all levels can have input into new strategic initiatives. That model will be based in part on what other companies in this book are now doing.

Aqua Engineers: The Next Step

Aqua Engineers, a Kauai-based water and wastewater utility engineering company, has a somewhat more formal process. Aqua Engineers was founded in 2001, it was sold to an ESOP in 2006, and has grown from 70 employees then to over 100 today. The founders controlled the board through 2011, and developed the first strategic plan in 2010. It was never used. A second strategic plan was started in 2013, but was never finished. It did, however, lead to a new CEO. The third strategic plan used a higher-involvement process and was implemented in 2016.

Ken Davis, Aqua's CEO, told our 2017 annual conference that the process of fits and starts on a strategic plan taught them not to start in an unhealthy management environment—the output may not represent the product of the folks who have to implement it. Using a much more collaborative process for the 2016 plan meant that there were detailed discussions, and, he said, those may be as important as the final product. "By being forced to discuss the future we had a clear vision of what is expected. Broadening the input early on gave a sense of ownership to the plan to a much wider group of employee-owners," he noted.

To start the new process, Aqua decided to get the help of an outside consultant. They considered an industry expert, an expert on issues in Hawaii, and an ESOP culture expert, ultimately deciding that what they most needed was the latter.

To kick things off, in early 2016, 11 managers held a retreat to identify five priority areas. From June through September, five teams with 28 participants did research and developed goals for five priority areas.

That included a survey of all staff. In October, the participants held a retreat to provide feedback on five priority area goals. That resulted in the goals being narrowed to three. Management then approved the goals and sent them to the board for final discussion and approval. Table 6-1 shows what was involved in each phase.

Table 6-1. Aqua Engineers strategic planning process

Phase	Identify big questions	Reconfirm mission, vision and values	Conduct external research & internal assessment	Set goals and strategies	Align and implement
Approves	Exec team	Board	n/a	Board	Senior leadership
Recommend	Exec team	Planning committee	Planning committee to guide process	Planning committee	Senior leadership
Consulted	Senior leadership and board	All managers and directors	All staff via survey external stakeholders	Managers and directors	Goal-setting meetings conducted in departments
Informed	All staff are regularly updated throughout process				

Recology

Given its size and scope, the high-involvement planning process at Recology less directly involves the broad workforce, but all workers have opportunities to share ideas.

Recology developed its first strategic plan by working with a major consulting firm. Julie Bertani-Kiser, senior vice president and chief human resources officer of Recology, told our 2017 NCEO conference that it was a "pretty plan," however, there was no buy-in from managers, the goals and objectives were unclear, and there were few metrics. This gave the executive team a starting point for what they wanted to do differently in the future.

In 2013, Recology decided to try a different approach. It used a bottom-up method to engage a cross-section of the organization to ensure a broad consideration of critical issues. Forty-five key employees participated in the process, and a consultant was used for high-level facilitation to rollout the second strategic plan in 2014.

Then in 2018, as the second Recology strategic plan was nearing completion with the goals being fulfilled, the company began planning its third five-year strategic plan. The planning started with the executive team's review of strengths, weaknesses, opportunities, and threats (SWOT), brainstorming possibilities, and creating a road map for the future. At this point, the board of directors weighed in with their support. From there, a planning team of 90 employees from three states came together to review the information, provide input, and ultimately create the goals associated with the plan. These employees were selected based on a process that included, but was not limited to, their expertise and/or interest in an area within the plan.

Teams were created to rally around a goal, and tasked to identify the strategies and tactics required to accomplish the goal. Through this process, the final implementation team of 50 employees (mainly management and professional positions) was selected to nurture the seed-goals from which Recology will continue to grow and develop in years 2019 through 2023.

A summary of the strategic plan was then mailed to each employee's residence in an effort to share with family how the company will develop in the next five years. To highlight this initiative, Michael J. Sangiacomo, president and CEO of Recology, has included a discussion of the strategic plan in his 2019 annual employee-owners' meeting presentation.

Tables 6-2 and 6-3 look at the roles and processes in the planning and implementation.

Julie Bertani-Kiser attributes the success of the 2014–2018 strategic plan and the creation of the 2019–2023 strategic plan to the process Recology put in place and the employee-owners involved throughout. In addition, the process allowed for the development of future leaders who would see the plan to fruition.

Bertani-Kiser stressed the importance of making sure employees have time to do their regular jobs, that there is collaborative software to facilitate communication, and that there be effective reporting tools.

Table 6-2. Recology strategic planning and process

Executive planning team	Planning team	Board of directors
Identifies core values, SWOT, and major issues impacting company and its future	Review strategic plan highlights from executives, provide input	Provide additional insights to executive team regarding future vision
Drafts potential major issues and goals	Work on creating the strategies and action plans on each goal	Approve strategic plan
Select planning team members who are designated to work on particular goals	Provide periodic updates to executive team for input.	
Kick off planning meetings		

Table 6-3. Recology strategic plan implementation and process

Executive planning team	Planning team	Board of directors
Select planning team members who are designated to work on particular goals	Provide periodic updates to executive management team	Review strategic plan progress annually
Kick-off meeting with implementation team	Track success through pre-determined KPIs (key performance indicators)	

Web Industries

Web Industries is a 100% ESOP-owned contract manufacturer based in Marlborough, Massachusetts. Started in 1969, the rapidly growing company now employs over 800 people in seven U.S. and three European plants. Web has grown more than 10% per year for two decades. It is one of the most financially and culturally successful ESOPs in the country. The company serves the aerospace, medical diagnostics, personal care, and wire and cable markets, often employing high-technology solutions. Web started as a relatively low-tech paper converter; its remarkable success has been a function of its ability to engage employees from the shop floor to management in finding innovative solutions to often complex customer needs.

Michael Quarrey, Web's vice president of operations, told us that "Web's high-involvement employee ownership culture makes everything we do better. The culture is both healthy and smart. The healthy part is based on our founder's belief that the 'essence of life is relationships.' This isn't just an epitaph inscribed beneath a portrait, although it is that, too. We teach employees the tools of emotional intelligence, teamwork, and conflict resolution. Building strong relationships is an expected behavior, a cultural norm, and something that everyone is required to do. Our culture of involvement also has a smart component: it is structured, there are clear methods and processes for participation, we can teach it, and everyone can learn how to do it."

Employee-owner involvement happens every day at Web in a variety of ways. The company's "Hoopla" process is ubiquitous: someone grabs a marker and a flip chart and asks: "What's going well; what's not going well; and what should we do differently?" Employees popcorn answers and the feedback drives improvement. Most Web locations have formal ideas teams that solve department-level problems. Based on the book *Ideas Are Free,* the ideas teams implement hundreds of ideas every year without the need for management oversight. Kaizen and Lean teams tackle larger problems, often resulting in very substantial improvements in cost, service, and quality.

The most advanced systems for employee involvement at Web relate to market strategy development and strategy deployment. In the mid-2000s Web decentralized market strategy development, the process by which the company chooses what services it will offer in which market segments. Moving the process from the corporate executives to market teams broadened participation to sales, operations, quality, technical, human resources, and financial staff at the manufacturing sites. Web recognized that these people have more direct knowledge and experience of markets, competitors, and internal capabilities and will therefore have better insight into strategic options and priorities.

Executives provide oversight and a market strategy process that includes all the normal elements including a survey of market trends, a critical assessment of internal capabilities and competencies, and sizing up of competitors. Explicitly using the model of seeking the adjacent possible (discussed earlier), the market teams develop strategic options and score these based on a set of objective criteria including:

- Segment size
- Growth prospects
- Capability fit
- Potential for innovation
- Competitive landscape / differentiation
- Degree of difficulty
- Alignment with other strategic options
- Financial uplift

The company uses a "stacking Swiss cheese" model to choose strategic options. Envision layering successive slices of Swiss cheese, each one representing one of the bullet points above. The strategy that works is the one where the holes line up.

Web's market strategy process is ongoing. The market teams refer to their strategy documents as "working papers" and update them routinely. The involvement of so many people in strategy development ensures strong alignment. Strategy is not handed down from the ivory tower, but developed bottom-up from the market teams.

Market strategies only point to new possibilities; they do not ensure success. Many brilliant corporate strategies fail because of poor execution and buy-in. Web's high-involvement systems for strategy deployment help address both issues. These efforts involve even more employee-owners in projects to drive specific strategic initiatives forward.

On employee ownership day in October, the plants divide into cross-functional teams for a strategy execution exercise. The teams each have a trained facilitator, but they do not have anyone from site leadership. The teams brainstorm projects in the context of the company's market strategy. They identify the ideas they think most merit pursuing, which may include some prior ideas that did not get adopted. They choose a spokesperson, often someone newer as a way to train people. At a general assembly, the presenters stand up and describe what the teams are recommending to management. The result can be 20 or more ideas, many of which will overlap because people have been doing this for years and have a good sense of what is possible and needed.

I had the privilege of observing this process at one of the Web facilities. The team meetings are made up mostly of machine operators. The discussion is at a very high level, informed by a working knowledge of the key metrics and a keen sense of the company's mission and strategy. The company-level meeting to review the ideas is similarly impressive. An observer who did not know who these people were might well assume they all had MBAs.

In November and December, the site leadership team considers the strategy deployment recommendations, chooses 3-5 key projects, and recruits "A3" teams to execute the months-long projects. (A3 refers to a paper size the ideas are recorded on.)

Over the next year, the A3 teams all use an A3 process to evaluate and track progress. Named for the paper size, the process is used in many companies as a way to chart the objectives, metrics, progress, and responsibilities in a project's implementation. Teams meet weekly, and once a month at a plant meeting, team reporters update all staff on each team's A3 progress.

The corporate office does not approve the ideas developed by the teams, but if the teams need significant capital resources to pursue the projects, they might need support from corporate.

An example: Web's medical team was facing slow growth in its traditional markets. The team developed a new market strategy to become a contract manufacturer of lateral flow test strips, used to test for infectious disease, pregnancy, food safety, and the like. The adjacent possible was adding reagent chemistry to the flexible materials Web had traditionally converted for diagnostics. This new market segment would elevate Web's offerings into a high growth area, would differentiate from competitors, and would take advantage of Web's automation knowhow—threading the Swiss cheese.

Once approved by executive leadership and the board, the market team created A3s to execute the strategy. One team focused on building out a "facility within the facility"; another on design and qualification of new equipment; and the third on upgrading quality systems for more rigorous FDA compliance. This effort has positioned Web with a unique offering and brought a strong pipeline of new opportunities.

Quarrey says the result of this is that "not only are our market strategies better because of wide employee involvement, but perhaps even more important, our strategy execution is more effective. Most companies' strategies fail in execution. At Web, we have market teams where all the employee-owners don't just know our strategy, but they know the whys and why nots, the whos and hows and whens and how muches. Having participated along the way in strategy development, it is hard to hold them back from gung-ho strategy execution."

High-Involvement Planning at SRC

The core concept of strategic planning at SRC is "people support what they help create." As SRC's founder and CEO, Jack Stack, describes it, "The way you produce the plan is just as important as the plan itself... To get ownership and ensure results, you must focus on how your plans are created and how people are involved in the process. Shifting the mindset from 'that's your plan' to 'this is our plan.'"

That means the best plans actively involve every employee. SRC calls its process "high-involvement planning" (HIP). SRC uses the HIP process to consistently involve, inform, and educate the entire organization on the realities of the marketplace and the company's strategy for growth.

There are four main steps in the HIP process: 1. create the plan, 2. communicate the plan, 3. commit to the plan, and 4. execute the plan. It's a framework for setting strategy, dealing with market changes, and enabling everybody to contribute. Each step reinforces the next. They work together to bring the plan to life. This is a repeatable process that, like a flywheel, gets easier to repeat the longer you commit to keeping it in motion.

Step 1: Create the Plan

SRC focuses first on creating plans that are rooted in reality. SRC believes that good strategies are primarily innovative, insightful answers to external (market, competitive) and internal (resources and financial) realities to achieve a goal. As a result, good plans have broad participation to provide the best possible understanding of those realities.

Four planning templates are used to create the plan.

- Sales and marketing planning template
- Strategy for growth planning template
- Financial planning template
- Succession planning template

The *sales and marketing template* helps SRC create a believable, predictable sales forecast. Because the sales forecast is the determining factor for so many other planning decisions (staffing plans, capital plans, inventory plans, product development plans, standard costs, production plans, etc.), SRC focuses a considerable amount of planning time on bringing the marketplace to their people to ensure there is a high level of confidence in the sales plan. SRC has used the following sales and marketing template for more than 30 years:

SRC Sales and Marketing Planning Template

- External opportunities and threats
    - — Economic, industry, market intelligence
    - — Competitive intelligence
    - — Customer intelligence
- Internal strengths and weaknesses
    - — Financial perspective; trends/benchmarks
    - — Stakeholder perspective; input survey
- Sales performance—five-year history/plan/actual/forecast
- Annual sales plan
- Growth and contingency planning
- Five-year sales outlook

- Our strategy for growth
- Buy-in

The *strategy for growth planning template* defines SRC's growth strategy, both long term as well as short term. What defines winning? Where will we play? How will we win? What capabilities do we need to win? The objective of the strategy for growth planning template is to answer these questions and define the long-term vision of the company as well as the strategies and actions we need to take today to move us closer to the vision. Objectives, goals, strategies, and measures are developed for one-, five-, and ten-year periods, as well as critical numbers for each period (table 6-4).

Table 6-4. SRC strategy for growth playbook

Long-term strategy		Short-term strategy		
10-year focus	5-year focus	1-year focus	3-month focus	Weekly focus
Shared purpose	Financial objectives	Financial plan	Financial forecast	Stake in the outcome
Shared vision	Objectives	Goals	Strategies and "rocks"	Measures
10-year critical numbers	5-year critical number	1-year critical number	Right drivers	Mini-Games™
Shared value	Value proposition	Growth and contingencies	Follow the action and keep score	

The objective of the financial planning template is to show the financial realities of the strategy. Does the strategy help us hit our financial goals? Is the strategy creating long-term value? Where are the vulnerabilities that need to be addressed? Where should we focus and invest to eliminate those vulnerabilities?

The *succession planning template* is focused on identifying the who. Who will execute the plan? Do we have the talent and the bench strength to execute the strategy and achieve our goals?

Step 2: Communicate the Plan

HIP breaks down the traditional annual planning and budgeting process used by many companies into a frequent communication rhythm that enables the organization to better respond to the changes in the market. This communication cadence keeps plans updated and dynamic—while also keeping people engaged and aligned with achieving those plans.

Using the planning templates described above, SRC establishes a review process that drives the planning cycle (table 6-5).

The key to SRC's planning process is its frequent planning sessions and weekly huddles to track, measure and report progress. For example, at SRC's huddles, leaders call on people to present their numbers, including performance and adjusted forecasts, plus any explanation of variance. That allows employees to follow the score and share ideas on how to improve. Employees all have ownership of line items discussed at the huddle. Huddles are where planning and the execution of the plan meet.

Step 3: Commit to the Plan

What makes the HIP process so effective is that it garners real buy-in from everyone in the organization by asking them to weigh in on how confident they are in the plan—not just the sales plan but also the contingencies and overall strategic direction of the company. It also gives everyone a chance to provide input and hash out any weaknesses they see in the plan.

As you can see from the planning rhythm described above, employee input and buy-in is baked into the cycle. Employees are asked for their input, and then SRC follows up with a plan. Before it is ratified, they ask for employees' confidence in the plan. This is used to gauge the effectiveness of SRC's communication and education of the plan, but most importantly the level of commitment to the plan.

Here are example questions from both the input survey and the buy-in survey:

Table 6-5. SRC high-involvement planning rhythm

	Ja	Feb	Mar	Apr	May	June	July	Aug	Sept	Oct	Nov	Dec
Sales and marketing plan					>>>				>>>			
Strategy for growth plan				>>>				>>>				>>>
Financial plan										>>>		
Succession plan						>>>						
									Employee input and buy-in			
Great Game of Business huddles	>>											

Employee Input Survey

1. What are the top two critical financial issues facing the company in the next six to twelve months?
2. What are the top two critical marketplace or customer issues facing the company in the next six to twelve months?
3. What are the top two critical operational or process issues facing the company in the next six to twelve months?
4. What are the top two critical people or culture issues facing the company in the next six to twelve months?
5. What should the company do better, differently, or more of?

Employee Buy-In Survey

1. What is your level of confidence in our sales and marketing plan? (0 = low; 10 = high)
2. What is your level of confidence in our strategy for growth and contingency plan? (0 = low; 10 = high)
3. What was your biggest takeaway?

Step 4: Execute the Plan

In the end, the final high-involvement plan is translated into everyday practices that will enable everyone to execute. Practices like critical numbers, bonus plans, mini-games, huddles, scoreboards, rewards, recognition, and education all support the process, as well as the continuous process of forecasting and re-forecasting to meet the goals. The plan is tracked, measured, and reported week in, week out. Deviations are identified, plays are developed, and actions are taken to meet (or beat) the plan. The execution of your plan now becomes everyone's focus, and they have the tools, education, and empowerment to act.

Clearly, this is a huge commitment of time and training. And equally clearly, it pays off. As noted earlier, SRC stock has grown by over 761,000% (that is not a typo!) since its ESOP was formed in 1983.

KEY TAKEAWAYS

People support what they create. The discussions around the plan may be as important as the plan itself. By being forced to focus on the future, team members have a stronger buy-in to the vision moving forward.

- Develop your key metrics at all levels to measure what you want to achieve.
- If you hire a planning consultant, decide up front what expertise they should have and what their role will be. Consultants should facilitate, not drive, the process.
- Strategic planning should include day-to-day work-level issues if they are causing problems or presenting opportunities.
- Get feedback early on in the process on goals, opportunities, and issues from all employees via a survey, focus groups, huddles, or other means.
- Develop a strategic planning rhythm with dates set aside for each step in the process.
- Make sure each element of the plan has an owner and a common reporting process.
- Make the process iterative, with employees moving ideas up the organization and leadership moving them back down and repeating the process.

CHAPTER 7

Governance

A Seat at the Table?

There is no requirement under ERISA for employees in an ESOP company to be represented on boards or have any other role in corporate management or governance. In a 2016 NCEO survey, 88% of respondents said they had one or more officers other than the CEO on the board, and 39% said they had a non-officer. While the survey did not probe that issue further, it is probable that most of these employees are there in some ESOP capacity, such as being on an ESOP communication or trustee committee. These employees may be appointed by the board, management, an ESOP communications committee, or an employee election. Seventeen percent of companies allow employees to vote for the board.

Companies that allow employees to vote for the board have traditionally found that employees are reluctant to run, although there are some exceptions. So if the board wants nonmanagement employees on the board, it usually has to reserve seats. Having nonmanagement employees on boards can have advantages. It sends a message to employees that this really is an employee-owned company. Nonmanagement participants can add a perspective on what is really going on at the workplace level. On the other hand, the employees have to take on the substantial fiduciary obligations of being a board member, learn to understand financials that may be unfamiliar, and learn about sometimes complex legal matters. Employees can learn to do all these things, but both they and the board must be willing to commit to the effort. In addition, many board members would be concerned that employees might be in a very difficult position if they choose to go against management on issues of compensation and strategy.

These arguments have kept the majority of companies from having nonmanagement employees on boards, although we have no research on whether the concerns are legitimate. But many companies have found ways to involve employees at the board level that stop short of full participation. These approaches allow boards to get meaningful input from people they would not normally encounter and provide employees an opportunity both to have that input and to see how the board process works. That can be an important step in legitimizing the ESOP to their peers.

This chapter looks at varying ways companies have included employees at the board or management level. There is only very limited research on whether having employees involved makes a difference in employee attitudes or corporate performance, and what there is suggests it has little effect in itself. The kinds of day-to-day involvement we have been discussing are clearly much more important. Nonetheless, for many companies, this kind of involvement does work and is seen as an essential component of their culture.

We also look at CEO performance surveys, another way for employees to have a role in corporate management by providing feedback to the CEO on issues that need addressing.

Explaining What Boards Do

Employees often have only a vague (and possibly incorrect) idea of what boards actually do, especially if there are outsiders on the board. Some employees think that the board really runs the company and the outsiders might not be the best people to do that. Others think that having a more formal board with outside experts makes the company stronger and employee ownership more meaningful. Many employees wonder why if they are owners, they don't have board responsibility. Because of these mixed perceptions, it is important for companies to explain what boards do and provide various ways for outside board members to interact with employees.

Start by explaining why employees are not represented on the board and/or employees cannot vote for the board—or why they can if you do. Each company will have its own take on this, but be diplomatically straightforward. If you have no employee involvement in a formal way, but do in an informal way (and you should!), explain that. Explain that boards have substantial fiduciary liabilities and personal exposure, and having outside board members is designed to act as a way to get expert input from people who can help the company grow. You may want to say that board duties are like other positions in the company and are designated based on specific sets of skills.

But also be clear about what boards do—and do not do. It is important for employees to understand that very few outside board members try to micromanage a company or override its leadership on business decisions, but rather serve to help leadership think about new approaches that companies might take.

On a more specific level, the board oversees the CEO, including compensation levels, performance, and succession. The board is responsible to the shareholders to make sure pay is reasonable, performance is at or above standards, and a sustainable succession plan is in place. The board approves the annual budget.

The board also selects and oversees the ESOP trustee to make sure that individual is doing what is required under the law and the plan, most importantly making sure the valuation is done properly to derive an accurate fair market value. The trustee also has the formal duty to elect the board. In practice, trustees almost always vote for nominees by the board.

The board is responsible for responding to serious acquisition offers. Should the board receive an offer at a substantial premium, if it decides that this is in the best long-term interests of the plan participants as shareholders (not as employees), it would forward the offer to the trustee to decide on what if any next steps should be taken. In practice, ESOP companies are rarely acquired unless they want to be. (Note in some states boards can take a broader view of what to consider, especially if they are B corporations.)

The board reviews and discusses strategic plans, operational issues, management issues, ownership communications and culture, and other ongoing business issues. Outside board members make suggestions and provide ideas, but only in the most extreme cases would outside board members seek to force a decision on management.

These high-level issues are not the stuff of the kind of idea-generation processes described in this book. These processes have a much greater impact on what the company does day-to-day, and employees need to understand these differences.

Varying Approaches to Employee Involvement at the Board Level

As noted, many ESOP companies do have nonmanagement employees on their boards, and the experience they report has been generally positive. Few companies have done as much to involve nonmanagement employees as has Carris Reels. Founded in 1951 in Rutland, Vermont, Carris became an ESOP in 1994. The ESOP became the majority owner in 2005 and bought all remaining stock in 2008. The company manufactures a variety of reels for the wire and cable industry as well as paper barrels, plastic barrels, and welding wire packages; and accessories, such as wire ties, caddies, and reel adaptors. It has 11 locations including Canada and Mexico. It has about 750 employees.

From its inception as an ESOP, former owner Bill Carris wanted to create a very high-involvement, democratic organization. An employee team actually helped design the terms of the ESOP, and elected committees function throughout the company. In addition there is a Corporate Steering Committee (CSC), which is made up of management and nonmanagement employee-owners who are dedicated to a wide range of issues and is primarily responsible for communications and decisions regarding governance, policies, benefits, and culture. The CSC also serves management and the board in an advisory capacity.

In 2014, a decision was made to include employees on the board. Dave Fitz-Gerald, CFO of Carris, says that "when there is an opening, we advertise internally for applicants. HR screens the applicants to confirm the criteria to serve are met. Then a subcommittee of our Corporate Steering Committee reviews the applications, talks with supervisors and HR at the employee-owners' site, and interviews the candidates." Based on the work of the subcommittee, the CSC names up to four candidates for consideration to be on the nomination slate.

The board of directors receives the vetted candidates, and the board in its entirety serves as nominating committee. The board as nominating committee then sends a slate back to the CSC, which will include the one candidate it selects to be added to that slate. The CSC then directs [by a vote among CSC members] the ESOP trustee committee to vote for the slate. The trustee committee meets to discuss the instruction they received, as a directed trustee, and to decide whether to follow the instruction. Then, at the annual meeting the trustee votes for the slate, as the sole shareholder. The experience so far, Fitz-Gerald says, has been very positive. "Non-executive employee-owners on the board have worked on and been a part of discussing and deciding major issues from acquisitions to compensation strategy, just to name a few. They represent a unique perspective, and they have a great record of making a difference in our company, and ensuring a more robust conversation."

CALIBRE Systems, Inc., an employee-owned management consulting and technology services company, has an ESOP committee that is elected by the workforce. The Employee Owners Advisory Committee's (EOAC) charter includes promoting a broad-based understanding of CALIBRE's ESOP and supporting a vibrant culture of employee-ownership. They have created thoughtful programs that link education to where people are in their employment lifecycle: information about eligibility for new employees, early diversification, and distribution rules for those approaching retirement.

One of the other functions of the EOAC is to elect one of its own members to serve on the board of directors of the company. The committee takes into account the person's tenure, his or her understanding of the business, and the suitability of the person's skills and experience to be a productive board member. As a director, that employee can provide insight into the concerns and ideas of the workforce, and often serves as a conduit for innovative ideas to travel from the workforce directly to the boardroom. Similarly, at NMR in Massachusetts, an ESOP-owned energy consulting company, the board, which has two outsiders, asked the ESOP Communications Committee to decide how it wanted employees to be represented on the board (elections, appointment by the committee, or some other option, as well as if the person should be voting or advisory). They ultimately decided they wanted a voting seat and for the person to be appointed by the committee. Board members also meet with two different employees at lunch at each meeting.

If a company adds one or more nonmanagement employees to the board, it needs to make sure that they, like every other board member, get the necessary training to do the job well, understand the fiduciary risks involved, and have the ability to understand financials. That most often involves having these employees sit in on webinars, read materials such as the NCEO's *ESOP Company Board Handbook*,[1] and go to conferences. Employees might often be excluded from some executive compensation discussions.

A halfway approach would be to have employees sit on the board in a non-fiduciary, non-voting capacity. At Barclay Water Management in Boston, CEO Don Carney started a practice of having the ideas team make a presentation at each board meeting. Carney believes this sends the right message to the team and the company that generating ideas from employees is the essence of an effective culture. The team takes about an hour to make its presentation. The ideas can often then be fodder for the board to think about strategic issues management might not have thought to raise. Barclay also invites two employees who have won a performance award to come for a short conversation with the board at each meeting. That provides additional recognition and a chance for board members to get a better idea of what day-to-day work is like in the company. At Radian Research in Indiana, the ESOP Communications Committee makes a 30-minute presentation on its activities for the year. CEO Tim Everidge believes this sends the right message to the committee about the importance of its activities. Board members can also meet with employees at lunches, ESOP days, and other events.

Employee Voting on Strategic Issues

New Belgium Brewery started its ESOP in 1999, when it had only about 60 employees, but it made employees owners prior to that with broad grants of phantom stock. In 1998 the company was considering

1. See www.nceo.org/r/board.

a switch to wind-based power. The company's management knew that projecting costs and assessing risks were a necessary part of making a good decision, but they also knew the analytical answer wasn't enough. Employees had to be on board. They would help pay for the additional cost because their bonuses would be reduced, and they would have to find solutions to the inevitable glitches involved in any major change. Simply making the right decision was not enough; the whole work force needed to believe in the decision.

To get broad support, a management team can take two general approaches. One is communication, explaining the advantages. The other approach, which New Belgium followed, is to involve the whole workforce in making the decision—that way the switch to wind energy would happen with employee support or it wouldn't happen at all. The company helped people educate themselves about wind power and let them weigh their own values. When the time came, the employees voted unanimously to adopt wind power. Making that decision by a vote required an investment of time and effort by everyone at the company.

The investment paid off in universal buy-in to the decision itself, and wind power is a success that New Belgium now integrates into the firm's public identity. The investment also paid off in larger terms: the wind-power decision was a moment of truth where people realized that their role at New Belgium is greater than simply being employees.

The New Belgium approach is rare even in ESOPs, but the idea of using a more formal process to get employee input into big decisions that will affect their jobs, while obviously coming with risks, also can have large rewards. At New Belgium, it was a seminal event for the company, which now has grown to over 700 employees—10 times the number when the vote was taken.

After the vote and the ESOP, New Belgium set up "POSSE," ESOP spelled backward with an extra S. It is made up of eight volunteers nominated by their peers and then elected to a two–year term via a popular vote on the company's intranet. In its early days, POSSE developed an introduction to ESOPs and presented it throughout the company. POSSE also spent months defining itself, including writing bylaws and a statement of purpose ("to foster a clear understanding of employee ownership while encouraging trust, belief and participation"). POSSE does more than education, though. To nourish the spark of participation created during the vote on wind power, POSSE looked at other issues, such as a sabbatical program, an issue that any employee would want to have input on. POSSE is also structured into the management and governance of New Belgium: its vice chair represents ESOP perspectives on the management team and its chair rotates in on the board of directors.

As this book was going to press, New Belgium's board had accepted a very attractive offer from the parent company of the Japanese company Kirin to buy New Belgium, and the employees have voted to accept the offer.

Employee Feedback on the CEO

Aside from participation at the board level, employees might also provide feedback on the CEO's (or other officers') performance. It takes a lot of confidence for a CEO to do this, but the feedback can be invaluable. It is essential that the survey be convincingly anonymous, perhaps even farmed out to someone who can provide the results to the CEO, such as a board member or consultant.

Below is a sample survey the NCEO developed for this use. It is based on a survey from the Thai stock exchange, modified by us for this purpose.

Sample CEO Evaluation Survey

This sample survey was developed by Corey Rosen of the National Center for Employee Ownership. Several of the questions are adapted from a publicly available source from the Stock Exchange of Thailand, which had the best set of questions Corey saw in an extensive search of sample CEO evaluation surveys. The others are based on questions ESOP companies have asked or that we added.

We suggest that each question should be answered with these options:

1. Performs well above expectations
2. Performs above expectations
3. Performs at expectations
4. Performs below expectations
5. Performs well below expectations

In addition, there should be a comment box for each option and a general comment section at the end.

Creating a Vision and Plan for the Company

1. [CEO name] has shown clear vision in correctly anticipating business trends, opportunities, and priorities affecting the company's prosperity and operations.
2. [CEO name] leads the company in setting philosophy that is well understood, widely supported, consistently applied, and effectively implemented.
3. [CEO name] has performed as an admirable role model for the organization.

Operations and Structure

4. [CEO name] has accurately identified and analyzed problems and issues confronting the organization.
5. [CEO name] has established an effective organization structure, ensuring that there is management focus on key functions necessary for the organization to align with its mission.
6. [CEO name] has organized and delegated work effectively.
7. [CEO name] has accurately supervised performance monitoring and performance control to ensure accountability at all levels of the organization.
8. [CEO name] has achieved the company's financial goals and market share targets.

Organizational Climate

9. [CEO name] is flexible and open to new ideas, welcomes feedback and criticism, and manages in a transparent style.
10. [CEO name] has motivated and encouraged high employee morale and loyalty to the organization, and facilitated teambuilding and cohesiveness among the company's employees to achieve the firm's vision.
11. [CEO name] ensures the ESOP culture is effectively communicated.
12. [CEO name] ensures that the company contributes appropriately to the well-being of its community and industry, and represents the company in community and industry affairs.

Strategy and Corporate Performance

13. [CEO name] has achieved the company's financial goals and market share targets.
14. [CEO name] has accurately identified and analyzed problems and issues confronting the organization.
15. [CEO name] leads in developing appropriate strategies for the company and in securing and allocating financial, technical, and human resources required for these strategies.
16. [CEO name] ensures the development of a long-term strategy that maximizes opportunities and considers risks, and establishes objectives and plans that meet the needs of customers, employees, and all corporate stakeholders.

General Comments

17. Name up to three things you think [CEO name] can improve on in the next year (be as specific as possible).
18. Name up to three things you think [CEO name] and/or NMR should focus on that are not necessarily a current focus right now.
19. Additional comments.

KEY TAKEAWAYS

- Make clear what the role of employees with respect to the board is and why.
- Employees on boards can provide valuable perspectives and credibility for the idea of being employee owned, but must be accompanied by careful training.
- If employees are not formally on the board, consider other ways to get employees involved in a non-fiduciary capacity.
- Consider doing a CEO survey.

Conclusion: Evaluate and Change

The process of getting to a high-involvement culture is an iterative one—you need to regularly reassess where you are and make needed changes. As people's involvement skills get better, systems that once worked will feel outdated and need changing. Even the best systems can get stale. Revitalizing your culture is hard work, but essential to success. The ownership advantage comes from ownership culture, and, like any improvement process at your company, measuring your performance helps ensure success. Most companies would not make a large investment without understanding the full picture, and making decisions on how to improve your culture is no different. Employee surveys are an effective way to ensure your ESOP committees are not flying blind in their efforts to improve various aspects of your organizational culture. They help assess strengths and weaknesses, engage employees, solicit suggestions, create actionable plans based on results, and measure progress over time.

You can evaluate where you are in a number of ways. Keep metrics on how many new ideas are being generated, where they are coming from, where they have fallen off, and which ones are working (and why those that are not working are failing). Your ideas team should regularly assess what these data mean.

Send people to conferences and other companies to learn what your peers are doing. Invariably, there are new ideas to pick up, and your employees will be energized by the process. If you are doing well, the bragging rights can renew a sense of purpose.

Focus groups are another good choice. The process described earlier of breaking people into random groups can be used here too to get people to identify a few key things that are not working and what might work better.

Finally, consider doing surveys. At the NCEO, we have identified five tips to ensure your survey strategy is effective:

1. *Begin with Action in Mind:* The planning process may take longer than you think. Consider not only what your company wants to measure, but also how to ensure you will be able to take action based on the results. Asking employees whether or not they are satisfied working at the company, for example, does not tell you what the company needs to do next. Effective surveys focus on specific aspects of your culture that can be improved upon, such as employee perspectives on how to find answers to specific questions, education and training, access to information, or their opportunities to engage in the business and provide input. Do the mental exercise of asking yourself what you will do if people agree with a question and what you will do if they do not. If there is no clear answer, you might need to rethink the question.
2. *Make It Comprehensive:* Other elements, such as demographic questions and written-response questions, can make your survey even more effective. Demographic survey items are questions that allow you to break the survey results down into employee subgroups based on tenure, age, department, location, or roles in management, for instance. This is especially important for companies with multiple locations, seeing as one location may have completely different needs or issues than another. While there may be fears among employees about how such items might be used to identify respondents, third-party survey administrators can help you ensure employee anonymity. Written responses can help add color to the quantitative results of your survey. You might ask a question such as, "What is the most important area in need of improvement at our company?" or "What can our company do to make you feel more like an employee-owner?"

3. *Be Honest and Transparent:* Results, especially negative results, can be overwhelming for companies, but do not fret. The point of the survey is to identify the most important areas in need of improvement. By soliciting the honest answers and perspectives of employees, you are presenting yourself with an opportunity and the first step toward improvement. Accept that the results are an honest reflection of your company's culture. Do not be afraid to share the results with employees and tell them exactly what your committee is planning to do to address specific issue areas. Doing so builds more trust in the process and shows you take the feelings of employees seriously. Not sharing the results may have a negative impact on employee attitudes and your company's culture.

4. *Create an Action Plan:* The worst possible outcome of employee surveys is a lack of action. If you conduct a survey and fail to respond to employee concerns, your company risks lowering employee morale and trust rather than improving the company's culture. Before starting a survey, commit to the hard work that follows. While there may be several issue areas that your company wants to focus on, trying to take them on all at once may result in no issue receiving sufficient attention. Some companies create a prioritized action plan that focuses on the aspects of their culture with the most negative responses. By addressing the most pressing issues first and fast, you show employees that you take their concerns seriously. During this stage of the process, it is also important to engage middle managers and involve them in the process of improving specific measures. Your team might ask managers of various groups to respond to specific results. Their insights will be important to understanding why certain measures are lower than others, and engaging them in the process from the start will help your team find the best ways to make improvements.

5. *Track Progress over Time:* The goal of your company's first survey is to measure current strengths and weaknesses, but surveying employees just once does not allow you to track progress over time. The most successful ESOP committees engage employees regularly.

Many do a survey annually, including open-ended questions. Your team should create a plan to ensure that the money and resources you spend on such initiatives are making progress over time.

Following these survey guidelines will improve the effectiveness of your engagement strategy. You can develop your own survey, or contact us for the NCEO's Ownership Culture Survey.

"There" Keeps Moving

Way back in the 1980s Cecil Ursprung joined Reflexite (discussed earlier) as its new CEO. The company had just become an ESOP. A friend asked him soon after how things were going, and Cecil said "We are about halfway there." Some years later, Reflexite employee-owners were on the cover of Inc. magazine as the entrepreneurs of the year. The award had always been just for an individual until Reflexite's employees collectively won it. Soon after that, his friend asked how he was doing again. "We are about halfway there," Cecil said. "But you told me that years ago when you were just starting," his friend said. "Yes," Cecil said, "but 'there' moved." There will keep moving, much like a seemingly receding rainbow you are driving toward. But like that drive, when you do it well, it is a beautiful journey.

Recommended Reading

Steve Baker and Rich Armstrong, *Get in the Game.* A great step-by-step guide to SRC's lessons on high-involvement management.

Amy Edmondson, *The Fearless Organization.* How to create a sense of psychological safety in workplace employee involvement programs.

Marshall Goldsmith, *What Got You Here, Won't Get You There.* Advice for leaders on how to be more open to new ideas.

Patrick Lencioni, *The Five Dysfunctions of Teams.* One of two very useful books on why teams sometimes don't work—and how to make them work better.

Harvey Robbins and Michael Finley, *The New Why Teams Don't Work.* Another good take on how to make teams work better.

Alan Robinson and Dean Schroeder, *Ideas Are Free.* A classic and practical guide on how to get more ideas from more people.

Jack Stack and Bo Burlingham, *The Great Game of Business.* The essential text on the most seminal, influential approach to management in the ESOP world.

Chade-Meng Tan, *Search Inside Yourself.* Google's text on emotional intelligence, self-awareness, and well-being—science-based, good for skeptics, practical step-by-step advice.

About the Author

Corey Rosen is the founder and former executive director of the National Center for Employee Ownership (NCEO) and now is its senior staff member. Corey has spoken on various subjects related to employee ownership all over the world with government, business, and union leaders, and he is regularly quoted in leading magazines and newspapers. He has appeared on national television and radio programs and also has authored four books on employee ownership, plus more than 100 articles for various business, academic, and professional publications. He has authored or coauthored several of the NCEO's practical and research publications.About the Author

About the NCEO

The National Center for Employee Ownership (NCEO) is a non-profit organization that has supported the employee ownership community since 1981. Our mission is to help employee ownership thrive. We have more than 3,000 members because we help people make smart decisions about employee ownership, with everything from reliable information on technical issues to helping companies reach the full potential of employee ownership.

We generate original research, facilitate the exchange of best practices at our live and online events, feature the best and most current writing by experts in our publications, and help employee ownership companies build ownership cultures where employees think and act like owners.

Membership Benefits

NCEO members receive the following benefits and more:

- The members-only newsletter *Employee Ownership Report.*
- Access to the NCEO's members-only website resources, including the Document Library, ESOP Q&A, and more.
- Free access to both live and recorded webinars.
- Discounts on books and other NCEO products and services.
- The right to contact the NCEO for answers to questions.

To join or order publications, visit our website at www.nceo.org or telephone us at 510-208-1300.

INDEX